THE COMIC

ADRIAN EDMONDSON

DAWN FRENCH

NIGEL PLANER

IN

Five Go Mad in Dorset WAR the beat generation

METHUEN in association with Channel Four Television Company Limited

PETER RICHARDSON

JENNIFER SAUNDERS

with Robbie Coltrane, Rik Mayall, Danny Peacock and Peter Richens

Bad News Tour Summer School and

"BACK TO NORMAL WITH EDDIE MONSOON"

First published in 1983
by Methuen London Ltd
11 New Fetter Lane, London EC4P 4EE
©1983 by Channel Four Television Company Limited.

Back to Normal with Eddie Monsoon ©1983
by Adrian Edmondson, Dawn French, Nigel Planer,
Peter Richardson, Peter Richens and
Jennifer Saunders

Book designed by James Campus

Filmset by Metro Reprographics Ltd, London
and printed in Great Britain
by Butler & Tanner Ltd,
Frome, and London

ISBN 0 413 53780 3

FOREWORD

They're all bastards!

Kirrin station.
A quiet country station. A steam train arrives. Julian, Dick, Anne and George (a girl) are peering out of a carriage window, waving madly, On the platform stands Aunt Fanny with Timmy, the dog and a black porter. The four children jump out. Each one is carrying two large suitcases.

ALL Hello Aunt Fanny!

AUNT FANNY Hello children.

ANNE It's really super to be on hols again Aunt Fanny.

GEORGE Oh Timmy! You're just as licky as ever.

    The porter loads their bags onto a trolley.

AUNT FANNY My word you've all grown so much.

JULIAN Thanks, old stick. Well it's great to see the girls again, isn't it, Dick?

DICK Rather!

    They walk towards the station exit.

"My word you've all grown so much."

AUNT FANNY Well I knew you'd all be ravenous after your journey, so I've prepared you a slap-up meal.

DICK Oh wizard! I'm starving.

JULIAN I vote we all have a cold swim first. I feel pretty hot and sticky after that train journey.

GEORGE Oh yes, lets!

They all climb into a black open Morris 8. The porter appears from the station pushing his trolley laden with bags.

DICK *(in a loud voice)* I say Ju, that man looks foreign.

GEORGE I expect his name's Golliwog.

ANNE *(laughing)* Yes, or Tarzan.

JULIAN I think we'd better call the police just as soon as we get back to Kirrin cottage.

ANNE Oh I'm so happy. I just know these hols are going to be really first rate!

    The car moves off down the lane. The porter follows on foot pushing the trolley.

". . . Anne's just a girl but she doesn't mind . . ."

Kirrin cottage.
The children are seated around a table piled high with food. Anne enters with the pudding.

DICK   Umm. Rhubarb tart, my favourite with lashings of cream.

GEORGE   You've had four helpings already, Dick.

DICK   Thanks, Anne. You really are a proper little housewife. Not like George. She still thinks she's a boy.

GEORGE   It's stupid being a girl. I wish I was a boy.

DICK   Oh really, George it's about time you gave up thinking you're as good as a boy. I mean Anne's just a girl but she doesn't mind, do you, Anne?

> *Anne shakes her head.*

GEORGE   Well I absolutely do mind actually.

JULIAN   Steady on, you two. The hols have only just started.

"Steady on, you two. The hols have only just started."

ANNE You seem so grown-up Julian.

Sweating and breathing heavily, the porter arrives at the garden gate with the luggage trolley. In the same instant a black police car with bells ringing pulls up beside him. The policemen jump out.

INSPECTOR Seize him, Sergeant.
>*They bundle him into the back of the car and drive off.*

The children are still eating. Aunt Fanny enters.

AUNT FANNY Well have you all enjoyed your supper?
ALL Rather!
AUNT FANNY I expect you're all ready for an early bed.
>*They all groan.*

GEORGE What was that very mysterious phone call, Aunt Fanny?
AUNT FANNY It was your Uncle Quentin!

"Your Uncle's been kidnapped again."

ANNE Yes, we haven't seen him yet. How strange!
AUNT FANNY As you know, he's a famous scientist and does a lot of top secret work for the government.
DICK Yes and I expect he's working on some new scientific discovery isn't he?
AUNT FANNY Well I didn't want to tell you, for fear of spoiling your holiday, but I'm afraid, children, your Uncle's been kidnapped again.
ALL Oh no! Bad show
DICK Crikey that must be a bit of a blow for you, Aunt Fanny.
GEORGE Yes, twice in six months.
AUNT FANNY Yes yes. Still I expect it'll all sort itself out in the end.
JULIAN Look here, Aunt Fanny. We were wondering. . .I mean, we don't want to be more trouble for you. . .
ANNE Yes go on, say it Ju!

JULIAN It's just that our bikes happen to be in first class order. So we thought we could all go cycling for a few days. I've looked at the map and there's rather an interesting ruined castle in Dorset we could look at.

AUNT FANNY Well I'm always worried that you're going to have another of those hair-raising adventures.

ANNE Oh nothing will happen this time, we promise. Anyway Julian will always look after us, won't you Ju?

AUNT FANNY Yes, I must say you do seem very. . .mature, Julian.

GEORGE So it's all settled then.

AUNT FANNY All right, I agree.

ALL Hooray!

Next morning. The children are outside the garden gate with their luggage strapped to their bicycles. The sea is in the background.

AUNT FANNY Well You've certainly picked a lovely morning to set off. Are you sure your brakes are in good order?

ANNE Oh yes the Highway Code is very strict about things like that and so are we.

JULIAN Well we're off now. Goodbye, Aunt Fanny.

AUNT FANNY Goodbye. Have a wonderful time.

GEORGE We will, don't worry.

ALL Bye bye.

       They cycle off down the lane.

The children are freewheeling down a road.

DICK It's a shame about Uncle Quentin.

GEORGE Yes I agree with you heartily, Dick.

DICK Still, now we can go absolutely mad if we want to.

ANNE Yes we can do anything. It's really first rate!

"Now we can go absolutely mad if we want to."

". . . fresh lettuce and lashings of ginger beer."

The children are seen cycling through the countryside. They stop on the brow of a hill overlooking rolling countryside and are having a picnic.

DICK I say, this is a jolly wizard lunch, Anne. You're really going to make someone a great little wife one day.

JULIAN Umm. My favourite. Ham and turkey sandwiches, heaps of tomatoes, fresh lettuce and lashings of ginger beer.

> *In the background two men, Rooky and Hunchy, are seen carrying a box across a field. They stop and start digging a pit.*

ANNE This is just the kind of holiday I like, picnicky meals and not too much adventure.

DICK Well don't speak too soon, old thing.

> *A black car draws up. A black-gloved hand throws out a piece of meat.*

MAN'S VOICE Here, Fido.

> *He drives off at speed. Timmy, the dog, gobbles the meat.*

GEORGE That's strange. Why on earth would somebody want to feed Timmy?

JULIAN Yes that was rather odd.

DICK Ssh. I say look over there.

> *They notice the two men digging.*

"What a strange pair!"

GEORGE What a strange pair!

JULIAN Yes one's got a big nose and thick lips and the other one's got mean, clever little eyes.

DICK And they're unshaven . Just look how they're slouching.

ANNE Urgh! Pooh! I hope they don't come near us . I feel as if I can smell them from here.

GEORGE Ssh. I can hear them talking.

HUNCHY What about the sparklers, Rooky?

ROOKY Don't worry, Hunchy, I'll take care of that.

HUNCHY Well now that you're out of gaol you'd better lie low.

GEORGE D'you think they're escaped convicts?

DICK Yes, or traitors to our country.

JULIAN We'd better call the police.

ANNE Oh look Timmy's fallen over.

> *Timmy is lying still in the grass.*

GEORGE Oh crikey, he's been poisoned!

JULIAN Never mind, George, we'll get another. Come on everybody let's find a telephone!

> *They cycle off.*

The children are now standing outside a phone box in a country lane. A black Wolsey police car with bells ringing pulls up. In the back are Rooky and Hunchy.

INSPECTOR Well done. Thanks to you we've caught these two red-handed.

JULIAN We're very glad to be of help sir.

INSPECTOR I must say you seem very grown up. I shouldn't be surprised if you join the police force some day.

JULIAN Thank you, sir.

ROOKY *(leaning out the back window)* You little bastard! I've just spent fifteen years of my life behind bars. *(The car moves off down the lane.)*

ROOKY *(shouts)* I'm going to kill you when I get out! I know where you live!

"You little bastard!"

DICK Phew!

JULIAN Well now let's stop in the next village and celebrate with some ice cream.

DICK Rather.

GEORGE I feel exactly like an ice cream.

JULIAN According to the map, there's a shop there that does some jolly decent ones.

The children cycle into the village of Heydon, very picturesque with a village green and shop etc. They go into the shop. a fat cheerful woman is handing out ice creams.

DICK Umm. This is grand.

JULIAN Yes I think we ought to pay you double price for these gorgeous ice creams.

    Julian hands her some money but she waves it aside.

WOMAN No no, young gent. I wouldn't hear of taking your money. But it's right down nice of you I'll be bound.

    Anne picks up a newspaper.

ANNE I say look at this, everybody. two more famous scientists have been kidnapped.

WOMAN Oh yes there's been a lot of strange comings and goings in this village, secrets and signs and threats . . .

    The door opens. Toby Thurlow, a rich young boy, enters.

  Hello, Master Toby.

TOBY Give me a chocolate cake and some ginger beer, old woman!

GEORGE You could say 'please'.

TOBY I'm so rich I don't have to. *(He hands the woman a five pound note.)* There you are, keep the change.

    He walks out.

WOMAN That's Toby Thurlow. His father's one of the richest men in the country.

GEORGE Well his son is certainly one of the rudest.

JULIAN I agree with you heartily, George. Well, we must be going. Thank you.

DICK Yes you really are a brick.

WOMAN It's a pleasure. Right down nice you are. Here, take these sandwiches and this cake with you. *(She hands them a huge pile of sandwiches and a cake.)*

As the children come out of the shop, Toby is astride his bike.

TOBY Hello, there.*(They ignore him and mount their bikes.)* My name is Toby Thurlow, you know.

GEORGE Yes we do know.

TOBY I say, you four look as though you're having a pretty exciting time. I think I'll come cycling with you for a bit.

GEORGE No thanks, we don't talk to other children.

TOBY Look here, I own this village, so you'd better be nice to me.

JULIAN Clear off with you before we call the police.

    He starts to move. Toby blocks his way.

TOBY Look, I didn't mean to be rude. It's all because I'm an only child and I'm stinking rich. I've never had any friends. You all look so decent. Please let me come with you.

GEORGE No we don't want you. Do we, Anne?

ANNE Well . . . he could stay with us for a short time I suppose, couldn't he?

"Give me a chocolate cake and some ginger beer, old woman!"

"That's Toby Thurlow. His father's one of the richest men in the country."

JULIAN What do you say Dick?

DICK Well if he promises to be good I suppose it wouldn't hurt.

JULIAN All right then, but you must do exactly as we tell you.

TOBY Oh I promise I'll do anything just to be friends with you.

They cycle off down the road.

More shots of the children riding through the countryside. They stop beside a slow-moving river surrounded by meadows.

JULIAN This looks like a grand spot for a picnic.

DICK Rather! I'm starving.

ANNE Me too!

GEORGE Hurrah. What's for tea Anne?

ANNE Ham and turkey sandwiches, bags of lettuce, hard-boiled eggs, heaps of tomatoes and lashings of ginger beer.

DICK *(screwing up his nose)* We're so greedy, aren't we.

TOBY *(looking at Anne)* You're pretty well-developed for a ten-year-old.

JULIAN *(studying the map)* I say, I think I've found a really first-rate spot to pitch our tents for the night. It's right beside a lake in some woods.

DICK Oh wizard! We can all go for a refreshing early morning dip. After all we *are* used to cold baths every day.

"You're pretty well-developed for a ten-year-old."

A black car pulls up. The same black-gloved hand throws out some meat for Timmy.

MAN'S VOICE Here, Fido.

He drives off again at high speed. Timmy gobbles the meat.

GEORGE That's strange. D'you think someone's got it in for Timmy.

JULIAN Yes that was rather odd.

TOBY I know who that was.

DICK Who was that and how do you know who that was? Come on tell us everything at once. We must know, because there's something very peculiar going on, that's for sure.

"Here, Fido."

TOBY His name's Dirty Dick. He was a bodyguard to my father and a right ruffian too. One day he had a perfectly furious row with my father after he kicked one of the dogs down a well.

GEORGE Erk! What a frightful beast!

DICK Well this is all getting very mysterious.

ANNE Oh dear I can feel another hair-raising adventure coming on.

The children ride through more countryside. They stop. Julian looks at the map.

JULIAN I think we're nearly there.

GEORGE Gosh we're simply miles from anywhere.

ANNE It seems so isolated. I'm sure some pretty queer things go on around here.

DICK Yes, look over there! There's a man parachuting into a field.

GEORGE So there is! Look.

JULIAN Maybe it's a spy being dropped into this desolate countryside or perhaps a deserter from the air force. That's even more likely.

GEORGE Come on, let's find out.

A rough track beside a field. The children creep over to the hedge. A black car is parked in a gateway.

DICK Look there's somebody here to meet him. It must have been pre-arranged.

They peer over the hedge and see two men, Red and Jake, digging in a field.

"I'm sure some pretty queer things go on around here."

ANNE Are they burying the parachute?

JULIAN No it looks as though they're digging something up.

The two men lift out a huge bomb from the ground.

DICK Gosh it looks like an atom bomb.

JULIAN So it does.

The men carry the bomb over to the car and sling it casually into the boot.

RED Good work, Jake. Remember don't spill the beans. You know what I mean.

JAKE Well now that we've done the dirty work, when do I get my money?

RED You'll get the money like I said. Just don't try and blackmail me, that's all.

JAKE Don't you worry about that. Secret information's my game.

They climb into the car and drive off.

ANNE This is all getting stranger by the minute. What can it all mean?

JULIAN Blowed if I know, but they're up to some funny business, I'll be bound. Come on, let's find this camp site before it gets dark.

GEORGE Yes and let's hope we don't come across any more queer happenings tonight. We've had quite enough for one day!

The camp site. Two tents have been erected in a clearing beside a lake.

DICK I feel pretty hot and sticky after all that! Anyone coming for a dip.

He takes off his shirt.

TOBY I will.

GEORGE Look here, isn't it time you were home now?

TOBY No thanks. I'm having too good a time here with all my new friends!

GEORGE Well I'm afraid there isn't much room for you. We've only got two tents. Where would you sleep?

TOBY I want to sleep with Dick.

GEORGE Julian always sleeps with Dick, don't you Julian?

"I want to sleep with Dick."

JULIAN *(appearing from a tent).* Yes it's time you scooted off now, Toby. You've had a long time with us.

TOBY I suppose Dick doesn't have any say in the matter.

GEORGE Look here, we're the Famous Five and that's the way it's going to stay. Besides you don't fit in.

TOBY Maybe not with you, you dike. *(Pointing to Dick)* But he wants me to stay.

GEORGE That's a lie!

TOBY Ask him.

GEORGE Do you Dick? *(Pause.)* Well?

DICK I . . . I don't know.

TOBY Ah ha! You thought you could get rid of me didn'ᵗ you! Well I'm going to be your friend for a bit longer!

GEORGE How can you be so feeble, Dick? You know perfectly well he's going to ruin the hols!

DICK It's not my fault, George. This whole situations's getting too involved for my liking!

   He stumps off in tears and stands sulking beside the lake.

JULIAN Look here, you've upset Dick now, you pesky little brat.

ANNE Can I do anything to help Ju?

   He squeezes her hand.

JULIAN No thanks Anne. You're a girl. I'd better do this.

ANNE You really are extraordinarily grown-up Julian.

JULIAN I know.

   He walks off towards Dick who is standing by the lake. Dick is still in tears. Julian puts a hand on his shoulder.

   What is it Dick?

DICK Nothing.

JULIAN Look, don't let the girls see you like this.

"This whole situation's getting too involved . . ,"

DICK I'm sorry, Ju. I didn't mean to let you down back there. It's just . . . growing-up feelings . . . and relationships, that's all.

JULIAN I understand.

DICK I mean what's so wrong with somebody wanting to be our friend anyway?

JULIAN There's nothing wrong about that. It's perfectly wizard but . . . what if everybody wanted to be our friend? Where would we be then? Umm?

DICK I don't know . . .

JULIAN Let's face it, Dick, we don't even know if he goes to a good school, and between you and I, he really doesn't look the adventure type.

DICK Adventures! Adventures . . . that's all we ever do! Always hearing secret conversations, digging up buried treasure, chasing people down tunnels! Why can't we do something else for a change!

JULIAN Like what?

DICK I don't know . . . just building model aeroplanes or country dancing.

> *Julian looks white with anger. Pause.*

"We don't even know if he goes to a good school."

JULIAN I'll pretend I didn't hear that!

> *He stomps off and smashes Toby in the face.*

Come on, George. You and I'll get some food from that lonely farmhouse.

> *Toby cries out in pain, blood pouring from his nose.*

GEORGE Oh shut up. Don't be such a cry-baby! You jolly well deserved that!

JULIAN Give him a bandage, Anne. Come on, George.

> *He storms off. George runs after him.*

George and Julian walk up to a lonely derelict farmhouse. The farmyard is full of blown safes, abandoned cars with bullet holes and the odd 'ROAD BLOCK' sign sticking out of the bonnet. Beside the front door there are one or two coffins.

GEORGE What a lonely place to live. No house for miles and no telephone, I expect.

JULIAN (*pointing to a car*) Look, that car's got no motor tax.

GEORGE Maybe it belongs to an illegal immigrant.

JULIAN I shouldn't be surprised.

He knocks on the front door. Sound of dogs barking. The door opens. It's Dirty Dick in a string vest and dark glasses.

DIRTY DICK Yeah?

JULIAN Good evening. We're the Famous Five and we're camping down by the lake and we need some food.

DIRTY DICK Eh?

JULIAN We'd like some free-range eggs, your own home-baked bread. Some of your own cured bacon and your honey and some tomatoes from your own garden would do splendidly.

DIRTY DICK Oh yeah, what d'you think this is, Harrods? Come on, piss off now and don't speak to any coppers about me.

JULIAN I don't take orders from you, whoever you are . . .

We hear the voice of another man, Fingers, from the inside the house.

FINGERS Who's out there, Dick? It's not the rozzers, I hope.

DIRTY DICK No just a couple of smarmy brats.

"What do you think this is, Harrods?"

FINGERS Well tell them to scarper. We've got some more dirty work to do.

GEORGE Wait a minute. You must be Dirty Dick.

DIRTY DICK No no. My name's not Dirty Dick, it's er . . . er . . . it's Dirty Douglas.

He turns to a dog barking inside.

Shut up Gnasher!

He kicks the dog. Sound of yelping.

GEORGE Oh don't! You hurt him.

DIRTY DICK He's my dog. I'll do what I like.

He kicks it again

JULIAN Look here, there's something very queer going on. *(He peers in past Dirty Dick.)* What exactly are you doing in there?

DIRTY DICK Oh so you've tumbled our game, have you?

FINGERS What's that! What's that! Are we done for, Dirty?

DIRTY DICK Sorry Fingers. I'm afraid we're bang to rights this time.

FINGERS Let's make a run for it, Dirty. You start the car while I grab the sparklers. We can still get away with it.

DIRTY DICK It's no good, Fingers. These kids are too darn clever for us. We'll probably get fifteen years each for this.

FINGERS Oh no! Not another stretch in clink. I'm going to take the easy way out.

    Sound of gunshot, and a body hitting the floor.

GEORGE What a horrid common voice he has. Ugh!

DIRTY DICK Oh well, I suppose I'd better go quietly down to the police station and get nicked, then.

The camp site. Dick and Toby are sitting beside the lake. Toby has his face bandaged. He groans in pain.

DICK I'm sorry about all this, Toby. I'm afraid it's all been a frightful mess. Julian didn't mean to hurt you. It's just that he takes our adventures very seriously. He's awfully sensible and grown up. *(Toby groans.)* And you must admit, he's got a wizard right hook.

TOBY My dad's going to sue him.

DICK Buck up, Toby. I think you're quite nice. Come on let's do something exciting under water.

    He dives into the lake. Toby watches. Two men suddenly appear from the bushes and put a sack over Toby's head, then carry him off.

Anne is arranging four logs around a primus stove. Humming to herself, she puts a name on each log. She picks up a feather duster and dusts the logs. Dick appears, dripping wet.

ANNE Oh do wipe your feet, Dick, I've just dusted there!

DICK My word you're a proper little housewife, Anne. It must be awful being a girl and having to do all the work.

ANNE Yes it would be nice to do some of the exciting things that you boys do. Still, I don't mind being dominated. At least I'm quiet and pretty, not like poor George.

DICK Yes that's true. I say is supper ready yet? I'm starving.

ANNE It will be when the others get back. Oh here they are!

DICK Hurrah!

    George and Julian appear.

"Serves him right for being *nouveau riche*."

GEORGE AND JULIAN Hello there!

JULIAN Sorry we're late, you two. We had a spot of trouble but we've managed to rustle up a hamper from the constable's wife.

GEORGE Yes she was a sweet old thing, gave us some cold turkey and ham, heaps of tomatoes, hard-boiled eggs, bags of lettuce and lashings of ginger beer.

DICK Oh wizard!

JULIAN I say where's young Toby got to?

DICK He's been kidnapped.

JULIAN Typical.

GEORGE Serves him right for being *nouveau riche.*

ANNE Yes and Jewish.

DICK Come on, let's tuck in.

The two tents are glowing in the dark displaying shadows of the children inside. Timmy's wagging tail is seen sticking out of the girls' tent.

GEORGE Oh Timmy. You're so licky!

ANNE You shouldn't let him do that George. It's not hygenic.

GEORGE We like it, don't we, Timmy.

TIMMY Wruff.

JULIAN *(from the other tent)* Come on, girls. Leave Timmy alone. Lights out, everybody. *(The tents go dark.)* Night night.

GEORGE Night night.

ANNE Night night, Julian and Dick.

DICK Night night, George and Anne.

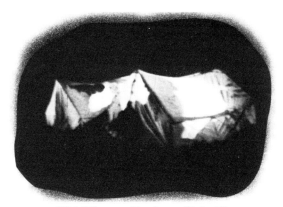

"Oh Timmy. You're so licky!"

Silence. In the darkness we see a match strike. Two hunchbacks, Knuckles and Lenin, are lighting cigarettes.

LENIN Right let's run through our evil plan once more, Mr Knuckles.

KNUCKLES Right you are Mr Lenin.

DICK *(inside the tent)* Wake up, Ju. I can hear voices.

JULIAN I can't hear anything.

DICK Listen there it is again.

KNUCKLES Bla bla bla bla – stolen plans – bla bla – missing scientists – bla bla.

LENIN Shh.

KNUCKLES Bla bla bla – atom bombs – bla bla – third world war – bla bla bla.

LENIN Ssh.

KNUCKLES Bla bla bla – Kneecap Hill – bla bla – big secret – bla bla – kidnapped boy – bla bla – everything ties up – bla bla bla.

LENIN Ssh.

JULIAN *(inside the tent)* I say, did you hear that?

DICK Missing scientists? Kneecap Hill? Big secret? What d'you think it all means?

JULIAN I'm not sure, Dick. But it all sounds very queer.

DICK Maybe it's some sort of clue.

JULIAN My word you're right! Come on let's get some sleep now! I'm much too tired to solve this mystery tonight.

DICK Me too!

"It all sounds very queer."

The next morning. Their tents are all packed away. The children are all poring over a map laid out on the grass.

GEORGE Well I can't see Kneecap Hill marked anywhere on this map. Are you sure that's what they said Dick?

DICK Of course I'm sure! You think I'm barmy or something!

JULIAN Steady on you two.

ANNE Wait a minute everybody! Look at this!

JULIAN What is it, Anne?

ANNE Well it's only a hunch.

DICK Go on, go on,

ANNE *(pointing at the map)* Look, there's a village here, Crutchley, and along here there's Thigh Woods.

GEORGE What about it?

ANNE Well this village down here is called Ankle On The Water, so maybe this hill here in the middle is Kneecap Hill.

JULIAN Gosh you're right, Anne!

DICK Good show. You're pretty smart for a girl!

GEORGE Fluke.

JULIAN *(folding up the map)* Come on! Let's find our way to Kneecap Hill as quick as ever we can!

The children are seen cycling through countryside once more. They stop beside an old man with a gypsy caravan which is parked on the roadside.

JULIAN Excuse me, Mr Gypsy. Can you tell us the way to Kneecap Hill?

GYPSY Oh you folks don't want to go up there, do you?

DICK Why is that?

GYPSY Well there's been some very strange comings and goings from the old ruin.

GEORGE An old ruin. How exciting!

GYPSY Oh yes. There's no phone, no gas, no electricity, no water laid on. Just secrets and signs and threats . . .

ANNE Ooh, I'm a bit frightened already.

GYPSY Oh you'll be all right young missy in that there short skirt and tight sweater. *(He moves closer to Anne.)* Ha ha ha! You remind me of my naughty granddaughter. Ha ha ha!

> *They move on quickly.*

"You remind me of my naughty granddaughter. Ha ha ha!"

GEORGE What a horrible gypsy!

ANNE Yes, he did smell rather unwashed.

DICK Come on, you two.

The children are walking along a track beside a high castle wall.

GEORGE How on earth are we going to get in? We'll never be able to climb over this high wall.

DICK Perhaps there's a secret way in. There always has been in our previous adventures.

ANNE Ugh! Not another big dark echoing tunnel full of . . .

JULIAN Ssh. Somebody's coming! Quickly everybody, hide in this ditch.

　　　　Knuckles and Lenin walk past, carrying a sack over their shoulders.

KNUCKLES Bla bla bla – Rio – bla bla bla – De Janeiro – bla bla.

LENIN Ssh.

KNUCKLES Bla bla bla – submarine – bla bla – leave it out – bla bla.

　　　　The children appear from the ditch.

JULIAN That's the same two men from last night.

DICK Yes they must have come out of a secret entrance in the wall down there.

　　　　They search along the wall. George finds a door-shaped crack in the wall.

GEORGE I think I've found it!

JULIAN Hurrah!

DICK I say you're pretty spunky for a girl, George.

GEORGE *(pleased)* Thanks, Dick.

JULIAN Oh blow! It won't open.

ANNE Maybe there's some secret mechanism that opens it.

JULIAN Of course! How silly of us not to have thought of that. *(He looks around. The track is surrounded by woodland.)* I say Dick, try bending that branch over there three times.

　　　　Dick goes to a branch and bends it. A door in the wall opens.

ALL Hurrah!

　　　　They climb in through the opening and feel their way along a dark passageway.

DICK Can't be much further to go.

GEORGE I wouldn't be surprised if this tunnel leads into a cupboard with a hidden room beyond. full of government secrets and strange machinery.

"– submarine – bla bla – leave it out – bla bla."

In the dark they push open a door into a cupboard then open another door into a room. The room is littered with empty jars of vaseline. Dick picks up a jar.

DICK Gosh, you're right, George. This must be their headquarters. We must be right inside the castle.

"Why if it isn't those nosey kids."

JULIAN I wonder where this leads to.

GEORGE Look! A foreign cigarette end!

> *Dick picks it up.*

DICK Yes and it's still warm.

JULIAN It must have been left here by some enemy of democracy, never expecting us to find it.

> *Lenin and Knuckles appear suddenly behind them.*

LENIN You're quite right. We never thought you'd stumble across our den of vice.

KNUCKLES Why if it isn't those nosey kids – bla bla.

JULIAN Yes we are very nosey indeed. And a good job too by the look of things.

KNUCKLES Well it looks as if those cheap foreign fags were a dead giveaway, Mr Lenin – bla bla bla.

JULIAN Now look here. Who's in charge of you ruffians? I demand we be taken to him at once.

LENIN Oh don't worry, you'll meet the boss soon enough. Then you won't be so cocky, young gent. Right, Mr Knuckles, I'll go first, you follow behind and if they make any trouble boot them!

KNUCKLES Right-i-ho – bla bla bla.

"Who's in charge of you ruffians?"

The children are shown into a large 'Brideshead Revisited'-type study. Toby is sitting in a high-backed chair, wearing a cravat and smoking with a cigarette holder. Knuckles and Lenin go out, shutting the door behind them.

ALL Toby!

GEORGE Are you all right?

DICK Have you been doped or tortured?

ANNE We've been *so* worried about you.

JULIAN Quiet everybody. Listen, Toby, we haven't got much time, so tell us quickly all that's been happening since you mysteriously disappeared.

DICK My word, it looks as though you've had a pretty frightful experience, old thing.

TOBY Well it was all a bit hair-raising at first, that's for sure, but now I quite enjoy it.

GEORGE What the blazes do you mean by that, Toby?

"Toby! . . . have you been doped or tortured?"

> *They hear a voice behind them. It's Uncle Quentin.*

QUENTIN I think I can explain everything, children.

> *They turn round. Uncle Quentin is standing in the doorway dressed in a smoking jacket. Beside him stands Mr Lenin.*

ALL Uncle Quentin!

LENIN Shall I stand outside, boss?

QUENTIN If you wouldn't mind, Mr Lenin.

> *Lenin goes out.*

Please sit down children.

> *They sit in a line on the sofa.*

JULIAN What's going on, Uncle Quentin?

DICK Yes, we thought you'd been kidnapped.

QUENTIN That was all part of my plan.

JULIAN What exactly do you mean, Uncle?

QUENTIN Well now that you dreadful children have found out my little secret, I suppose I might as well spill the beans.

DICK You mean the kidnap was all a hoax? Whatever for?

QUENTIN For many years now, your Aunt Fanny and I have not had a proper marital relationship. She is an unrelenting nymphomaniac and I'm a screaming homosexual.

"Toby and I are fleeing the country tonight."

(The children look at each other, puzzled. He takes Toby's hand.) It seemed quite pointless to try and explain this to you, you little prigs, so we concocted this story to save your Aunt from any further embarrassment. Anyway, there's nothing you can do about it now, because Toby and I are fleeing the country tonight in a fishing boat.

GEORGE But what about the stolen bomb? Dirty Dick? The two scientists? And the poisoned meat?

QUENTIN Oh that was all just a ruse to try and throw you off the scent. They were all third-rate movie actors employed by me.

JULIAN *(standing up)* Well you're wrong about one thing, Uncle Quentin. There *is* something we can still do and that's call the police. Homosexuality is still against the law in this country, as well you know it.

"It's no good, Uncle Quentin, you're a queer."

QUENTIN   Oh dear. I thought that even you, Julian, might show a morsel of sympathy and understanding to your dear old Uncle. Just for old times' sake.

DICK   *(standing up)* It's no good, Uncle Quentin. You're a queer and that's the end of it.

> *Sound of police bells. George and Anne stand up.*

ANNE AND GEORGE   Hurrah! Here come the police.

Outside the ruined castle. Toby and Uncle Quentin are seated in the back of a black police car. The Inspector is shaking the childrens' hands.

"It'll be quite some time before they see the light of day again."

INSPECTOR   Well done, Famous Five. We've had our eye on these two for quite a time now, and thanks to you, we've caught them red-handed. It'll be quite some time before they see the light of day again. You're certainly the kind of youngsters we want in this country. I'm proud to have met you. *(He salutes them.)* Good luck to you, Famous Five.

> *He gets in the car and drives off.*

DICK   Well that was an adventure and a half.

GEORGE   Who would have thought that about Uncle Quentin?

ANNE   *(hugging herself)* Urgh! I'm glad he's been safely locked up. I never did like him one bit anyway.

JULIAN   Well I think after all that excitement we deserve a slap-up meal, don't you?

DICK   Rather. I'm starving!

GEORGE   What a superb idea.

"You're certainly the kind of youngsters we want in this country."

DICK Cold ham, turkey, heaps of tomatoes, bags of lettuce, hard-boiled eggs and lashings of
      ginger beer!

ALL Hurrah!

They mount their bikes and cycle off down a track, and can be heard talking as they go.

ALL Look here . . . I say . . . Gosh . . . Phew . . . There's something very queer about . . . First rate
     . . . My word . . . Right down nice you are . . . Well this is grand . . . Frightful . . . I'll be bound
     . . . Buck up . . . Thanks, old stick . . . Oh blow . . . I agree with you heartily . . . Just as licky as
     ever . . . Rather . . . You are a brick . . . Thanks old thing . . . What about the sparklers? . . .
     Hair raising . . . Bad show . . . Lashings of ginger beer . . . Wizard . . . Hurrah . . . .

Written by Peter Richardson and Peter Richens

CAST					
JULIAN	Peter Richardson	SERGEANT	Barney Sharpe	DIRTY DICK	Ron Tarr
DICK	Adrian Edmondson	MAN IN CAR	Robert Richardson	FINGERS	Nosher Powell
ANNE	Jennifer Saunders	HUNCHY	Nosher Powell	KNUCKLES	Nosher Powell
GEORGE	Dawn French	ROOKY	Ron Tarr	LENIN	Ron Tarr
AUNT FANNY	Sandra Dorne	WOMAN IN SHOP	Robbie Coltrane	GYPSY	Robbie Coltrane
PORTER	Marcus Ford	TOBY THURLOW	Danny Peacock	UNCLE QUENTIN	Ronald Allen
POLICE INSPECTOR	Raymond Francis	RED	Ron Tarr		
		JAKE	Nosher Powell	Directed by Bob Spiers	

England under occupation, 1985

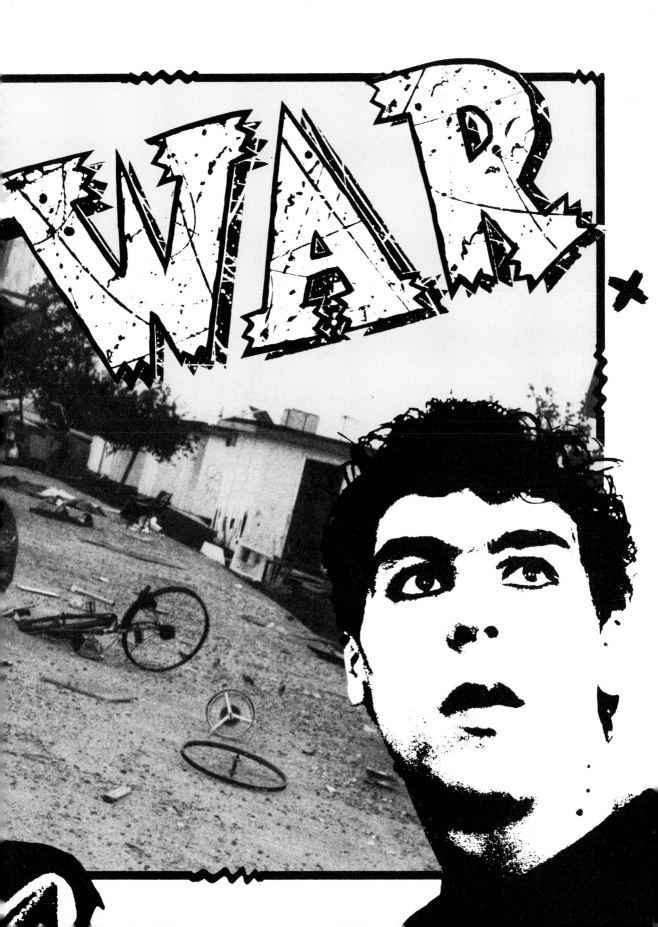

A SCRUBLAND TRACK BESIDE PYLONS. SOUND OF SYNTHESIZED FUNK MUSIC. A LEOPARD SKIN-COVERED CHEROKEE CAR SUDDENLY APPEARS AND DRIVES PAST.
A VIEW OF BUMPY TRACK SEEN THROUGH THE WINDSCREEN OF A CAR. THERE IS FUNKY MUSIC PLAYING ON THE CAR RADIO WITH A 'TONY BLACKBURN' TYPE DJ.

DJ OK. Right . . . er, we've just heard that the Warsaw Pact countries invaded Surrey at dawn this morning so there may be a few delays on cross-channel ferries, OK. More news on that later.

Godfrey, a young Steve Strange type, is driving. Beside him is Hermine who is in tears, sniffing.

GODREY Cheer up darling.

HERMINE This bloody war has really pissed me up.

GODFREY That's all behind us now, Hermine. I think we're going to love it out here, in the middle of nowhere. *(He looks around him)* Just the two of us.

HERMINE No more friends, no more pop music concerts, no more buckets of fizz at the Venue.

GODFREY Don't be silly, Hermine. We can learn how to mix our own cocktails.

HERMINE I love you, Godfrey. You're so together.

GODFREY Don't worry, darling. Everything's going to be OK. Look, there it is.

The cherokee appears through a gateway and crosses a field to a bungalow. Godfrey and Hermine jump out. Godfrey is carrying a bag of MacDonald's hamburgers.

GODFREY What d'you think, darling?

HERMINE Oh, it's just like you said. It's so tacky, so tasteless. *(She embraces him)* Oh, I love it.

GODFREY Let's go inside and eat our hamburgers.

They go into the bungalow. Panning away from the cottage, we see four soldiers sitting in the middle of a field opposite.

THE SOLDIERS ARE FOUR BLIND ENGLISH-TYPE COMMANDOS. ONE OF THEM, MICK, IS POURING TEA INTO THE GRASS, MISSING THE FOUR CUPS EVERY TIME.

MICK Tea up, lads.

> *They fumble around and pick up an empty cup. Each soldier doesn't want the others to know he's blind. Slug cannot find his cup.*

SLUG Where's my cup?

MICK *(pointing in the wrong direction)* What's the matter, you blind?

SLUG Why do you keep saying that?

COCKER Look, stop arguing you two. We've got to find a way out of this wood.

SLUG Wood? What wood?

MICK Wood! You know, trees and bushes . . .

SLUG I know what a bloody wood looks like . . . I'm a fucking commando . . .

TOMMY Ssssh.

MICK What was that?

> *They all look around in silence.*

See anything, Tommy?

TOMMY *(looking around)* No.

> *Cocker pretends to empty his cup*

COCKER Ugh. This tea's awful. Hand me a can of beer, somebody.

MICK Here you are, Cocker.

> *Mick hands him a grenade. Cocker pulls the ring. Explosion.*

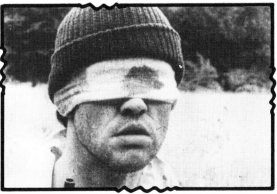
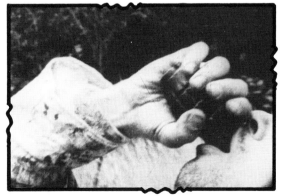

INSIDE THE BUNGALOW. GODFREY IS EATING A HAMBURGER. HERMINE IS READING THE SUN NEWSPAPER.

HERMINE What was that?

GODFREY What?

HERMINE That big bump.

GODFREY Maybe it's something in the cellar. I'll go and have a look.

HERMINE Shall I come with you?

GODFREY No, you stay here, Hermine. I'd better go down there . . . alone.

> *Godfrey goes out. She picks up the newspaper. Front page picture of mushroom cloud. Headline: 'GOTCHA'.*
>
> *The four blackened soldiers are outside the bungalow. Cocker has climbed a ladder onto the bungalow roof and tied a rope to the top of the ladder. Tommy is half-way up the ladder.*
>
> *Mick and Slug are feeling their way along the wall of the bungalow to the front door. They are all muttering: ''WHO DARES WINS''.*

MICK Ready.

COCKER Ready.

> *Slug throws a smoke bomb into the garden, as Mick kicks open the front door. Simultaneously Cocker slides down the rope, knocking Tommy off the ladder. They land in a pile by the front door.*
>
> *Mick and Slug burst into the bungalow coughing.*

MICK Get your hands up. Move!

> *He smacks into a wall.*

SLUG Nobody move! Stay where you are!

> *Tommy and Cocker appear from behind.*

TOMMY Everybody against the wall!

COCKER Get down, Trevor! That's a tone of voice you don't question.

> *Hermine does not move. She watches them feel their way past her around the kitchen, pointing their machine guns in all directions. Slug opens the fridge door and throws a grenade in and quickly shuts the door. Hermine runs out of the kitchen, slamming the front door behind her. The soldiers instantly machine-gun each other.*
>
> *Hermine looks in horror at the bunglow as the fridge blows up. A shower of eggs, milk, sausages and butter lands on her. She runs off across the field.*
>
> *She clambers up over a ditch onto the road.*
>
> *Meanwhile Godfrey, dazed and blackened, appears at the front door of the bungalow, eating his hamburger.*

GODFREY Hermine! Hermine!

> *He runs to the car.*

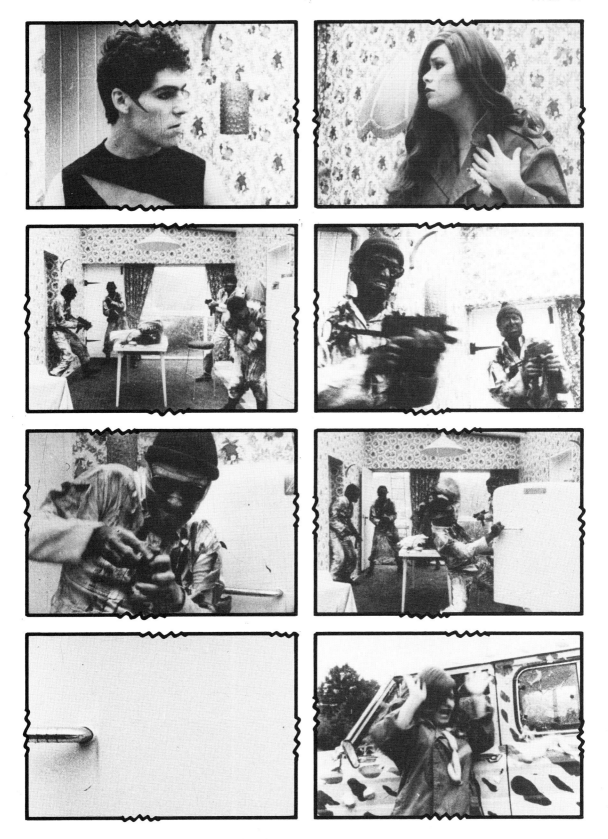

HERMINE IS STAGGERING ALONG A COUNTRY LANE. A LARGE ESTATE CAR COMES DOWN THE ROAD AT SPEED, ALMOST KNOCKING HER OVER. THE CAR SCREECHES TO A HALT. A SALESMAN GETS OUT.

SALESMAN   Hi! Feeling run down? Nervous about your future? Well, who isn't? Are you embarrassed by flaky skin, massive hair loss or internal bleeding?

> *He goes to the back of the car and opens the boot.*

Well, Progarb has something to show you.

> *He pulls out some plastic suits from a box.*

Many housewives are finding normal protective clothing drab and unexciting. But now thanks to Progarb you can have safety with style.

> *He holds one up.*

The Bianca. A very fetching two-piece survival suit in Surrender White, with matching helmet and booties.

> *Hermine discreetly opens the driver's door and gets in.*

Or for that very special occasion, there is the Widow, a very nice off-the-shoulder disaster gown . . .

> *She drives off.*

. . . complete with dolby stereo and personal plumbing.

GODFREY IS DRIVING ALONG A TRACK. THE CAR RUNS OUT OF PETROL. HE GETS OUT AND LOOKS ACROSS THE SCRUBLAND. A LONE TENT STANDS IN THE FIELD. IT HAS 'US ARMY' WRITTEN ON THE SIDE WITH A US FLAG ON THE ROOF. OUTSIDE THE TENT SIT A GENERAL AND WALLY IN A JEEP. THEY ARE STUDYING A MAP.

GENERAL OK, so we're here. What's this blob here?

WALLY That's Ireland.

GENERAL Umm. Ummm. OK, let's go over this again. My name's General Erwin and I live at 222 Marine Drive, Washington D.C.

WALLY Correct.

GENERAL OK. Now this is where I get lost. The President has sent me from here . . .

WALLY Washington.

GENERAL Er . . . OK. Across this blue stuff . . . to this brown stuff.

WALLY That's Europe, General.

GENERAL OK . . . let's get this down.

He writes it in his notebook.

GENERAL Now. What about all those other guys?

WALLY Er . . . what guys, General?

GENERAL Those guys that all dress the same. You know, the ones that came with us.

WALLY You mean the troops.

GENERAL Er . . . the troops, yeah, ummm, ummm. Tell me, Wally. How do they fit into all this?

WALLY They fight the enemy.

GENERAL OK. Er . . . do they know about this?

WALLY Well, they just do what you tell them, General.

GENERAL Gee, that's nice of them.

WALLY Will that be all, General?

GENERAL What do you think?

WALLY I think that's everything.

GENERAL OK.

> *Wally goes to the hut.*

Oh, Wally.

> *He pulls out a handgun.*

When do I use this?

> *Wally has disappeared. The General sees Godfrey.*

Hey, boy.

> *He fires the gun.*

I'm General Erwin. I live at double two three Marine Drive, Washington. Where do you live?

GODFREY Not very far from here. I'm . . .

GENERAL Spell 'communist'.

GODFREY Er . . . C.O.M. . . .

GENERAL You ever seen one?

GODFREY I don't er . . .

GENERAL Well you can't miss 'em. They're big red fellows with shifty eyes. They go round speaking funny and screwing people's sisters . . . of course, they wouldn't screw my sister. You seen my sister? *(He pulls out a photo.)* Oh. That's the dog. Wait a minute.

GODFREY Excuse me, General, I'm looking for my wife. She's gone missing.

GENERAL Is that in Europe?

GODFREY She's disappeared.

GENERAL You'd better speak to Wally. He's in the hut.

> *Godfrey goes to the tent and opens the flap.*
> *The tent is dark and smoky. The soldiers – Chas, Doc and Hatchet, are sitting round a table. Doc is loading one bullet into a gun.*

DOC OK. Place your bets, boys and girls.

CHAS Hey, I'm going for the big one. *(She puts two cigarettes on the table.)*

HATCHET Your big chance, Chas.

> *Chas notices Godfrey.*

CHAS Who are you?

GODFREY I'm Godfrey.

DOC This your first time in 'Narm?

GODFREY Pardon?

HATCHET You wanna sit in?

DOC Yeah, come on.

GODFREY Oh well I'm . . .

DOC Playing. Sit down. Got some cigarettes?

GODFREY Er . . . I've got a pipe. *(He puts it on the table.)*

ALL Hey! Hey! Hey!

> *They all up their bets. Doc hands the gun to Chas, who spins the chamber and points it at her own head.*

CHAS Where you from, kid? *(She pulls the trigger. Clunk.)*

GODFREY *(in a high voice)* Islington. *(He clears his throat)* Er . . . Islington.

> *Chas hands the gun to Hatchet.*

HATCHET Ever seen a dead baby?

> *He pulls the trigger. Clunk. He hands the gun to Godfrey, who has sweat pouring off his face.*

GODFREY I can't do it. I can't do it. Oh no mother, wake up. Where are you?

> *They're all looking at him. He looks at each in turn, swallows hard, then with hand shaking he points the gun at his head. He pulls the trigger. Clunk. They all cheer. Doc takes the gun, and spins the chamber and points it at his head.*

DOC There you are, kid. There's nothing to it.

> *BLAM. He blows his head off. Godfrey is covered in brains.*

CHAS Phew!

> *She collects the bets. Godfrey gets up shakily. A hand pushes him back into the seat. Another GI screwball stands over him.*

SCREWBALL Don't get up for me, kid. *(He pushes Doc's corpse off the chair.)*

Is this a free space? *(He sits down and looks hard at Godfrey.)*

Hi. My name's Screwball. You got a wife and kids?

GODFREY Just a wife. Well, fiancée.

HATCHET Ever been to the States, Godfrey?

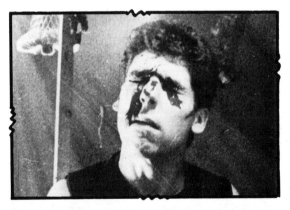

GODFREY *(loudly)* Oh, yes. I've been to Chicago.

> *Screwball points the gun at Godfrey's temple.*

SCREWBALL Shut the fuck up! Shut the fuck up! I'm going to kill the motherfucker!

HATCHET Hey, steady, Screwball.

CHAS He's got a sister in Chicago.

> *Screwball glares violently at Godfrey as he points the gun at his own head. He pulls the trigger. Clunk. Still glaring, he hands hands the gun to Hatchet. Hatchet puts a pack of two hundred cigarettes on the table.*

HATCHET *(to Godfrey)* Don't mind Screwball. He's just a bit upset.

> *He pulls the trigger and blows his head off. Wally comes in. He pushes Hatchet off the chair.*

WALLY Anyone sitting here?

CHAS OK. Place your bets.

SCREWBALL Hey, let's play another game. Pass the parcel.

GODFREY *(with huge relief)* Yeah!

    Screwball pulls out a hand grenade.

ALL Yeah, woo hoo!!!

    They all place bets. Screwball pulls out the pin and hands it to Godfrey. Godfrey is frozen with horror and just gapes at the grenade. Wally snatches it and hands it to Chas. They all go 'OOH' as they pass it on to the next. The grenade starts to fizz as Godfrey passes it again to Wally. He gets up and makes for the door. He runs out of the tent as the grenade explodes. The General is still in the jeep reading his map.

GENERAL Hey, boy. Come and look at this.

    Godfrey walks over to the jeep. The General fires his gun.

GENERAL What are these squiggly things here?

GODFREY They're roads, General.

GENERAL OK. OK. And these blotches. What are they.

GODFREY They're towns.

GENERAL OK. I think I'm getting the hang of this. Now what about this green patch?

GODFREY Er . . . it's a golf course.

GENERAL That's what I wanted to hear. *(He fires his gun.)* Come on, let's go.

    Godfrey climbs in the jeep. they drive off.

HERMINE IS DRIVING SLOWLY ALONG A DUSTY TRACK. THROUGH THE WINDSCREEN WE SEE REFUGEES COMING TOWARDS HER, PUSHING PRAMS FILLED WITH COLOUR TV'S, VIDEOS, MICROWAVE OVENS AND RUBBER PLANTS. SHE STOPS THE CAR, GETS OUT AND FIGHTS HER WAY THROUGH THE CROWD TOWARDS A SMOKING, EMPTY SHANTY TOWN. HERMINE WALKS SLOWLY UP THE MAIN STREET. IT IS FULL OF CHALETS AND BROKEN NEON SIGNS. SOUND OF WIND. BLUE SKY AND WISPS OF SMOKE. SHE STOPS OUTSIDE A RUN-DOWN CAFÉ.
CLOSE SHOT OF SOME SPURS JANGLING.
HERMINE SEES TWO UNSHAVEN MEN STANDING UP THE ROAD. THEY ARE CARLOS AND MIGUEL. BOTH HAVE YELLOW TEETH AND PHONEY SPANISH ACCENTS.

CARLOS & MIGUEL Ha, ha, ha, ha, ha, ha, ha.

> *She turns and sees two more of the same, Julio and Mario standing down the road behind her.*

MARIO & JULIO Ha, ha, ha, ha, ha, ha.

> *She runs into the café. A waitress is wiping a table as she enters.*

MARILYN Hello, dearie. Pot of tea for one, it it?

HERMINE Can I use your phone? It's an emergency.

MARILYN What's the matter, dear?

HERMINE There's people running out of the village and four men dressed like Mexican cowboys with guns and . . .

MARILYN I know, it's the same every day, darling. Rape and pillage and looting . . . I don't know.

HERMINE But Mexicans? I don't understand . . .

MARILYN No they're not Mexicans, darling. They're local. Nice boys, really. You know, a bit high-spirited. Of course, they do watch a bit too much television.

> *Outside the main street is deserted. Sounds of breaking glass and breathy laughter.*
> *Close shot of a finger pushing the 'PLAY' button on a cassette recorder. Sound of Spanish heavy metal music.*
> *A noose is seen being tied around the head (from behind).*
> *A mannequin dressed in 'Take Six' – type clothes is being hoisted on "the gallows". The "Bandits" are laughing. There are three mannequins strung up. Miguel, the leader, paces up and down in front of the mannequins, shouting to the empty village.*

MIGUEL This is what happens when you take the piss with Miguel. Ha. they think that Miguel is just a stupid peasant. They say, 'Ha ha Miguel wears flared trousers'. They say Miguel got no CSE's.

> *He spits.*

I spit on your punk rock.

> *He looks at a mannequin and slaps it.*

Stop hanging about. Ha ha ha!

> *The others all laugh loudly. A leg falls off. Miguel holds up his hand.*

Carlos. Give me droga.

> *Carlos pulls out a jagged mirror and lays down a line of Harpic. Miguel writes out a cheque, rolls it up and snorts the Harpic. He looks around with a manic drugged look.*

Umm. That makes me feel *bad*.

> *Julio tries to open the door of an electrical shop. He takes a few paces back, then runs head first through the door. He puts on a pair of headphones, finds a radio, switches it on and looks for the earphone socket.*

RADIO DJ Well the missiles are really raining down on London at the moment and we have a competiton for you now. The first person who can get out there and spot an SS15 gets a free Radio 'Get Down' T-shirt, OK. So . . .

> *Julio casually drops the radio and picks up a smaller one.*

SECOND RADIO . . . in the panic and hysteria that followed, many hundreds of people were killed and this has caused severe tailbacks on the M6.

> *Julio switches on a blender and puts the radio in it. He picks up some small batteries and puts them in his cartridge belt, then picks up a TV remote control gadget and points it at six TV's. They all show the same pictures.*

TV COMMENTATOR   . . . and in between the exciting bouts of action, Toyah Wilcox, the Forces' sweetheart, keeps our boys in the groove. Get on down, Toyah.

Julio places two pocket calculators in a toaster.

MARIO IS WALKING AROUND THE VILLAGE SUPERMARKET, WITH AN EMPTY BASKET. HE PICKS UP THINGS, THEN PUTS THEM DOWN. AT THE FREEZER HE PICKS UP A YOGHURT, THEN CHANGES IT FOR A DIFFERENT FLAVOUR. HE STOPS AT THE CASH DESK, PUTS THE YOGHURT IN A PLASTIC BAG, PULLS OUT A FIVE POUND NOTE, OPENS THE TILL AND GIVES HIMSELF THE CHANGE PLUS A RECEIPT.
JULIO APPEARS FROM THE ELECTRICAL SHOP CARRYING A HUGE PORTABLE STEREO BLASTING OUT SPANISH MUSIC. HE IS WEARING A BANDOLIER FULL OF TRANSISTOR RADIOS. HE STANDS ON THE PAVEMENT AND LAUGHS LOUDLY.
MARIO IS WALKING ALONG THE PAVEMENT EATING HIS YOGHURT. HE HEARS GUNFIRE AND LOOKS UP. JULIO IS PULLING OUT A TRANSISTOR RADIO, SWITCHING IT ON AND THROWING IT IN THE AIR. MIGUEL FIRES AND MISSES. JULIO THROWS UP ANOTHER. CARLOS FIRES AND MISSES. LAUGHTER.
INSIDE THE CAFÉ MARILYN AND HERMINE ARE DRINKING TEA.

MARILYN   . . . and of course, love, all the middle classes are selling up and becoming refugees, so trade isn't very good at the moment. I would have gone myself, but I'm a bit stuck you see. I've got eight kids and they've all gone down with this funny er . . . bone cancer you get and er . . . both me parents are crippled so I *am* a bit stranded.

Pause.

Still, you gotta laugh, haven't you?

MIGUEL AND THE OTHERS Ha ha ha ha.

> *Hermine and Marilyn turn to see the 'BANDITS' standing in the doorway.*

MARILYN Oh, hello, Donald. How's your mum doing?

MIGUEL My name's not Donald – it's Miguel.

MARILYN All right, darling. What can I do for you?

MIGUEL *(he spits).* Pot of tea for four, you bitch!

MARILYN Tch. He's a lad, isn't he?

> *She goes out, humming. Miguel walks over to Hermine's table. Swivels a chair round and sits down.*

MIGUEL My name is Miguel. I kill communists . . . with my teeth. *(He smiles. Yellow teeth.)*

HERMINE Is that why they are so yellow?

MIGUEL *(nervous laugh. Pause)* You like salsa?

HERMINE It's OK.

> *He snaps his fingers. Julio switches on the huge cassette player and blasts out Latin American music. They jig about. Miguel looks at Hermine's foot, she starts tapping it. He smiles, then snaps his fingers. The music stops.*

MIGUEL You hear that? It's the people's music. Communists don't like salsa. They only like to read big books with no pictures . . . I know these people. They think they can walk in here with no ''Excuse me please boys – here's the revolution''. *He strikes a match.*

Ha. Well, they are going to have to speak with Miguel first.

He lights a huge cigar. A large army truck draws up outside the window with 'COMMUNISTS' written on the side. Miguel chokes on his cigar.

CARLOS   'Ere, bugger me, Donald. It's the bloody Russians. What am us going to do?

MIGUEL   *(in normal voice)* Quick, out the back way. Run like fuck.

They collide with Marilyn carrying a tea tray. It crashes to the floor. The door opens and Ivan, a handsome blond Russian soldier enters.

IVAN   Good afernoon. I hope we're not disturbing you?

MARILYN   Oh no, love. Come right in. D'you want tea? How many are there of you?

She peers out the window.

IVAN   About fifteen thousand.

MARILYN   Is that all with sugar?

INSIDE A US TRANSPORT PLANE THE GENERAL AND GODFREY ARE SITTING OPPOSITE SIX MEAN, TOUGH COMMANDOS IN THE JUMP BAY. THEY ARE ALL PLAYING WITH KNIVES, STABBING THEMSELVES AND EACH OTHER. THE GENERAL IS SHOWING GODFREY SOME PHOTOS.

GENERAL   . . . and this is my neighbour's dog.

BOLSEN   We're approaching the target, General. The men are ready to go.

GENERAL   Er . . . OK. Bye. *(To Godfrey)* This is our lawn. All this green stuff is grass.

Bolsen opens the plane door. The men stand up.

BOLSEN OK men. You're the toughest, hardest, cruellest, stupidist guys in this whole goddam war, and don't forget it.

The first soldier, McClowsky, prepares to jump out.

Hey, McClowsky! Where's your parachute?

McCLOWSKY Parachute? What the hell do you think I am, Bolsen?! Parachute's for cissies.

He slaps Bolsen across the face, then jumps out. Another soldier, Brown steps forward.

BROWN We're the Fighting Fifth, Bolsen; we ain't playing kids' games.

He slaps Bolsen, then jumps. A third soldier looks at Bolsen with contempt, then throws his parachute on the floor and jumps out. The others do likewise.

A COMMUNIST JEEP MOVING ALONG THE ROAD. IVAN IS DRIVING. HERMINE IS HANDCUFFED BESIDE HIM.

GODFREY, WITH PARACHUTE, HAS LANDED ON SCRUBLAND. NEARBY THERE IS A BAMBOO CAGE WITH A PRISONER INSIDE. HE WALKS OVER TO THE CAGE. INSIDE THERE IS A STARVING MAN WATCHING A WATER DRIP ON A COLOUR TV. HE STARES AT THE MAN.

MAN *(faint)* Help me. Help me.

Godfrey tries to open the cage door but gives up.

GODFREY What can I do?

MAN Change the channel.

Godfrey hears the voice of a Japanese Sergeant, Harry Kiri, behind him.

KIRI You like cage, yes? Very nice. We get from Habitat.

*Godfrey looks around and sees a group of Japanese Soldiers wearing Sony headphones.
Harry Kiri has a row of pocket calculators in place of medals.*

GODFREY Where am I?

KIRI You are in the canton of Mitzebushi, formerly Milton Keynes. We here to protect consumer of Japanese product. You come with me yes please.

A JAPANESE FACTORY COMPOUND WITH WIRE FENCE. GODFREY IS LINED UP WITH SEVERAL OTHERS, FACING HARRY KIRI, WHO IS STANDING ON A PLATFORM IN FRONT OF A PRE-FAB WEARING A SONY WALKMAN.

KIRI My name is Kiri. Harry Kiri. Haw, haw. Old Samurai joke.

No reaction.

Ah. Where is famous British humour now? Answer – in Tokyo. John Cleese very big in Japan. Now you all work very hard like dogs. If you very good, you work for five years and get pocket calculator. *(Tapping his row of calculators.)*

AN AUSTRALIAN What about some food, you yellow bastard?

KIRI Food make you fat. Very bad for spirit of work. Japanese work twenty-six hours a day and live in cupboard with mother-in-law. She so thin, when she cross the road to feed chicken, her arse fall in river. Haw, haw, haw. Oh yes. Very old Japanese joke . . . Any question?

One of the prisoners collapses. A north country man, Hovis, steps forward.

HOVIS Excuse me, your Imperial Highness.

KIRI *(removing headphones)* Pardon?

HOVIS With reference to er, rule twelve, paragraph three, as er, shop steward, I officially withdraw my labour.

KIRI Very well, Mr Hovis. You spend two weeks annual holiday now in car boot.

He clicks his fingers. Two guards also wearing Sony Walkmans take Hovis to the corner of the compound. There is a mound with a car boot sticking out of it, surrounded by a barbed wire fence. They open the boot.

AUSTRALIAN Good luck, Pommy.

HOVIS Vote Labour.

Cheers from the prisoners. The guards shut him in the boot.

KIRI Anyone else for annual holidays now?

THE PRISONERS AND GODFREY ARE WORKING ON THE PRODUCTION LINE, WHISTLING THE THEME FROM "BRIDGE ON THE RIVER KWAI". GUARDS WALK UP AND DOWN.

TWO BRITISH OFFICERS ARE TALKING FURTIVELY.

FIELD MARSHAL Jenkins.

JENKINS Yes, sir.

FIELD MARSHAL We've got to do something to help the war effort. We've got to slow things up.

JENKINS Yes, sir.

> *They look around warily and give signals to the others. They all start whistling at half speed.*

ALL THE PRISONERS ARE FILING INTO THEIR HUT. HARRY KIRI STANDS IN THE DOORWAY, WITH A TRAY OF TEA. HE BLOWS A WHISTLE.

KIRI Time for tea-so-strong-filthy-spoon-stand-up-in-it ceremony.

> *He goes out. The Australian goes to a crack in the door and peers out. He gives the thumbs up.*

AUSTRALIAN OK. Let's go.

> *They all spring into action. Two men unscrew the front of a 'Space Invaders' machine and disappear through it.*

You coming with us, Godfrey?

GODFREY Are you digging a tunnel?

AUSTRALIAN Too right, digger. We've just built ourselves a whole bloody subway system.

> *He turns round a map of the London Underground and points at it.*

We're linking up here with the Northern Line.

GODFREY That's amazing!

AUSTRALIAN You'd better meet Jenkins and get togged out.

> *They go to the other end of the hut.*

This is Godfrey, sir. He wants to come with us.

JENKINS Hello.

AUSTRALIAN When you've finished here, go and see the Captain over there.

> *He goes. Jenkins picks up a list.*

JENKINS Right. What do you want to be, Godfrey? Guard or commuter?

GODFREY Er . . . I'll go as a commuter.

JENKINS *(studying Godfrey)* Ummm. You look the young executive type to me. Probably lives in Morden, er . . . drives a Volvo estate and beats his wife at weekends. You know the sort.

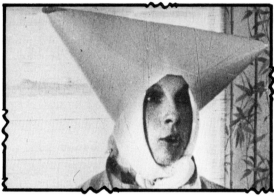 

He hands Godfrey a bowler hat and a brolly.

Had a bit of a job with this one. Made it out of old Marmite pots, ha.

GODFREY   It looks very real.

The Australian, with headband and guitar, comes over.

AUSTRALIAN   How does this look, sir?

JENKINS   Well, you should pass as a busker. Yes, should be all right. Show me one of your busking tunes, corporal.

AUSTRALIAN   *(sings)* 'Let me take you by the hand,
                                And lead you through the streets of London . . .'

JENKINS   Yes, yes. That should do the trick splendidly. Remember to keep your eyes on the ground and sing through your nose. That way you should be all right. Next.

A Field Marshal wearing tartan cheese cutter and scarf steps forward.

Ah, Field Marshal. How are you doing with your Scottish football fan?

FIELD MARSHAL   *(pretending to be drunk)* Eh! Two-nil, you bastard.

He nuts Jenkins.

JENKINS   Well done, sir. That should do the trick.

Godfrey is talking to the Captain.

CAPTAIN   Right, let's go through this again. A guard approaches you in the train and demands to see your ticket. What is your reaction.?

GODFREY   I say, er, ''Go back to where you came from, you black bastard''.

CAPTAIN   Very good. Now. Here's one ticket to Pinner, one brown paper bag with bondage photos and one copy of . . .

A man by the window makes a 'Space Invaders' start signal.

MAN Deedle doo da.

> *The signal is repeated all down the hut to the 'Space Invaders' machine. Two men standing beside it spring into action and pretend to play the machine, making all the rocket and explosion noises. The others rush around concealing things. Harry Kiri enters. The prisoners all act over-natural. Two are playing a fast game of chess.*

FIELD MARSHAL Checkmate. Your move.

> *Jenkins and the Captain are singing and dancing a funky disco number. One is pretending to be the director.*

JENKINS AND CAPTAIN 'Get down on that funky beat,
> Get on down that funky street . . .'

CAPTAIN No, no, sir. It's 'Get down *on* that funky beat'. Let's do it again.

> *Harry Kiri looks around him. Satisfied, he walks towards the door. He stops and sees a yellow tube ticket on the floor. The hut goes silent. He picks it up and turns to Godfrey.*

KIRI What is this yellow thing?

GODFREY Er . . . custard.

KIRI *(looking at the ticket)* Ah. Oxford Circus custard. Famous English delicacy. *(He puts it in his mouth.)* Umm. Tastes like Mother's Pride.

> *He goes out. Jenkins slaps Godfrey on the back.*

JENKINS Phew. Well done, Godfrey. That was pretty close.

AUSTRALIAN Yeah . . . never thought he'd swallow that one! *(He laughs loudly.)*

JENKINS Look, we'd better move fast. There's very little time to lose.

OUTSIDE IN THE COMPOUND HARRY KIRI AND TWO GUARDS OPEN THE CAR BOOT. HOVIS CLIMBS OUT BLINKING.

KIRI Now you ready for work, yes?

> *Hovis spits at Harry Kiri. The guards stick him back in the boot.*

THE MEN ARE LINING UP BESIDE THE 'SPACE INVADERS' MACHINE. ALL HAVE DIFFERENT HATS AND PROPS, BUT ARE STILL IN PRISON CLOTHING.

JENKINS Everybody line up and have your tickets ready.

CAPTAIN Good luck, sir.

JENKINS And you, too, Captain.

CAPTAIN Well, you all know what to do. All I can say now is: 'Good Luck, and hope to see you all at the Wimpy Bar in Piccadilly Circus. The milk shakes are on me!'

ALL Hurrah! Thanks, sir.

CAPTAIN Right, open her up, Roland.

> *Roland opens the front of the 'Space Invaders' machine, revealing an entrance to the Underground with adverts, etc.*

AUSTRALIAN Hey, Captain. The Nips are coming!

JENKINS Quickly now.

> *They all clamber through the machine.*

NIGHT. A RUSSIAN BORDER POST NEAR LEICESTER SQUARE. SOME RUSSIAN SOLDIERS STAND BESIDE THE TRUCK MARKED 'COMMUNISTS'. BEHIND THE BORDER POST THERE IS A SIGN SAYING: "YOU ARE NOW ENTERING THE NEUTRAL ZONE OF SOHO".

MARKOF *(swigging vodka)* So this is swinging London, comrade. Hah. We have massacred half of Europe to get here. I personally have killed and seriously injured twenty-four people to be here.

ZARKOF Me too.

MARKOF And for what? *(He looks through the fence)* Where is Elton John? Where is the mini skirt?

ZARKOF Where is 'On the Buses'?

> *Pause.*
> *They turn a spotlight on the neutral zone. Two cider drinkers, a man and a woman stand blinking in the white light.*

THE TWO DRUNKS Daniel is leaving tonight on a plane. Da da da da to Spain . . . youp.

ZARKOF What do you want, derelict comrades?

> *They simultaneously stretch out a hand.*

DRUNKS Give us a quid. Youp.

IVAN AND HERMINE ARE WALKING ALONG THE PAVEMENT IN THE WEST END PAST A THEATRE SHOWING A RUSSIAN BALLET.

IVAN I'm in love with you, Hermine. When this war is over, I want you to come back with me, to the Soviet Union.

HERMINE Oh, I'm so confused, Ivan.

IVAN Everybody has the wrong idea about my country, Hermine. It's a very happy place. There's no masturbation, no vandalism. no drug taking – *(Pause)* and no wife-beating.

HERMINE So what do you do when the pubs close?

IVAN Is it really so hard for you to embrace world socialism, darling?

HERMINE No, no, I think that communism is really super.

IVAN So what is your confusion?

HERMINE I'm in love with another man.

They stand under a street light. We see the feet of a corpse hanging over their heads.

IVAN Why don't we look on the bright side, darling. He is almost certainly dead.

GODFREY IS SEEN RIDING UP AN ESCALATOR ON THE UNDERGROUND.
IVAN AND HERMINE APPROACH THE CHECKPOINT, ARM IN ARM. THEY STOP AT THE
BARRIER. HE SALUTES THE OTHER SOLDIERS.

IVAN Will I see you later tonight?

HERMINE If you like.

IVAN I'll meet you here, then.
  He kisses her.

HERMINE I'd better go now. I mustn't be late my first day of work.
  They kiss again. She walks through the barrier into the neutral zone.

IVAN Yes, we have a saying in my country: bad time-keeping leads to an early death.
  She gives him a wave and a smile. The two drunks appear out of the darkness. They stretch out a hand.

DRUNKS Give us a quid.
  She clutches her bag. One steps forward.

DRUNK Youp . . .
  There is a gunshot. The drunk drops dead. Hermine looks at Ivan who is holding a gun. He smiles and waves.

IVAN Night night, sweet comrade.
  She gives a nervous smile and runs off.

THE ENTRANCE TO PICCADILLY CIRCUS TUBE STATION. GODFREY COMES OUT OF THE UNDERGROUND AND LOOKS AROUND AT THE LIGHTS, THEN HEADS TOWARDS THE WIMPY BAR.
INSIDE THE WIMPY BAR A SWEATING, UNSHAVEN TERRORIST, BREATHING HEAVILY, PACING UP AND DOWN, ACCOSTS GODFREY, WHO IS QUEUEING.

TERRORIST   Do you believe in God?

GODFREY   Er, yes.

TERRORIST   You wanna be famous. Ha ha ha.

GODFREY   Er.

TERRORIST   *(hands him a plastic bag)* This is for you. *(He goes out laughing.)*
         Godfrey reaches the counter.

GODFREY   French fries and a milkshake, please.
         He stares at the girl behind the counter. It's Hermine.

HERMINE   Godfrey! Oh Godfrey!

GODFREY   Hermine!
         They embrace.
      I love you!

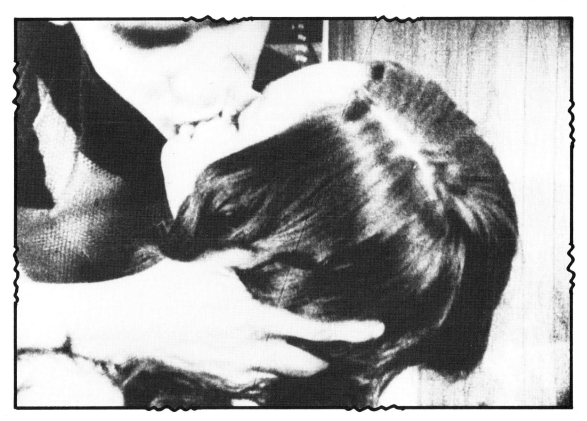

They kiss. The plastic bag is around Hermine's shoulders, ticking loudly.
Blackout.
Ticking sound.
Sound of alarm clock ringing.
Explosion.

Written by Peter Richardson and Peter Richens

CAST

Robbie Coltrane
Salesman, Screwball, Mario, Harry Kiri, Markoff

Robert Davies
Carlos

Adrian Edmondson
Mike, Hatchett, Julio, Bolsen, Man in Cage, Jenkins, Zarkoff

Dawn French
Hermine

Rik Mayall
Slug, General, Hovis

Danny Peacock
Godfrey

Nigel Planer
Tommy, Doc, Ivan, McClowsky, Australian

Peter Richardson
Radio DJ, Cocker, Wally, Miguel, Brown, Field Marshall, Drunk, Terrorist

Jennifer Saunders
Chas, Marilyn, Captain, Drunk

Directed by Bob Spiers

the beat generation

A pale sunrise over the sea. In the foreground there is a long sandy beach. Over the sea. Sound of be-bop improvised saxophone playing.

We see a large white half-timbered shabby house by the sea. It has a balcony, a porch and french windows, that lead onto an overgrown garden in the foreground. Desmond, a young rich house owner and weekend hipster, appears through the french windows. He stands posing in front of the house, then saunters over to a washing line. There are a dozen pairs of sunglasses hanging from it. He selects one, goes to a window and looks at his reflection. He musses his hair, turns away from the window, then spins around to see himself again, frowns uncertainly, then looks down the garden.

A black sax player leaning against a white telegraph pole at the end of the garden nods approvingly at Desmond. Desmond puts on a cool face and saunters over to a hammock strung between the verandah posts. With cool care he climbs into it and arranges himself in a casual pose. The camera pulls slowly back showing the house, the garden and a road in the background. There is a long pause. All looks quiet and peaceful. Then the hammock collapses.

Jeremy an angry young man is furiously driving along in a Ford Zephyr. The front passenger seat is empty. In the back are: Alan a successful underground poet and Eleanor, a young middle-class swinger, wearing a fur coat and high heels.

Alan is smoking and Eleanor is "scat" singing. The background is the open road.
The car is seen speeding along a straight road.
Eleanor lets out a scream and clutches her head.

eleanor– I'm going berserk. These weekends are so wild, Alan, just driving anywhere we like with so many crazy artists and poets like you and Kix. It's such a trip . . .

      She screams and looks out the window.

    What's it feel like being a success, Alan?

alan– Sucess? Well, it's like . . er . . going to an orgy in clean underpants.

eleanor– Oh wow!

alan– It's Marlon Brando throwing up in your bathroom.

eleanor– Oh crazy!

      She continues singing.
      The car on the move. Sound of kazoo and singing.

Outside a transport café and garage. Kix, a freeloader and armed poet, wearing a mohair suit and T-shirt, is outside the café. He puts a penny in the bubble gum machine and nothing happens. He starts banging it.
The car is passing through suburbs.
Kix is prising the machine off the wall with a jemmy. The car draws up behind him.

eleanor– Kix!

> The bubble gum machine comes away from the wall with a crash. He picks it up under his arm and quickly gets into the back of the car. They drive off.
> Jeremy is sweating with anger, his jaw muscles clicking. He changes gear viciously, about three times in two seconds. In the back with Alan and Eleanor, Kix is trying to lever open the machine.

eleanor– Hey Kix man! Crazy!

kix– Hey Alan I writ this crazy love poem for you, Dig this.

eleanor– Yeah dig it!

kix– Er . . . Bang bang she was dead
      I'd shot her through the head.

alan– Ummm. You really are the most promising illiterate of our generation, Kix.

> The machine bursts open, spraying bubble gum everywhere.

kix– Gum, anybody?

The car on the open road.

eleanor's voice– Write a poem about my legs, somebody.

alan's voice– Which one?

eleanor's voice– What d'you mean which one?

kix's voice– The beautiful whore called Peg
        The Venus with one leg

alan's voice– The only woman I ever loved.

    Inside the car Eleanor screams and sticks her tongue in Kix's ear.

eleanor– I'd cut it off for you, Kix.

alan– Honey you'd just fall over.

    Jeremy is breathing hard and grinding his teeth. He punches the dashboard.

    On a straight open road we see the car approaching. It starts to swerve, then screeches to a halt – sideways across the road. Pause. Jeremy gets out and slams the door. He walks ten yards up the road and spits viciously onto his woolly jumper. He goes back to the car and kicks the front tyre then turns his back on the car, sulking

eleanor– He is *so* angry.

    Jeremy gets back into the car, slamming the door again. The car takes off with a screech of burning rubber and disappears up the road.

At La Fellatio, a ritzy London restaurant. Charles, a dapper publisher and Alan's literary manager, is having lunch with Kurt a German businessman. In the background people and cars are passing. Charles stirs his coffee and hands Kurt a copy of Alan's book, *Famous Cocktails*.

charles– This is a copy of Alan's latest. I think you're going to love it. Now I know I've said all this before, Kurt, but this one really is totally obscene. I mean it's probably *the most* vile, disgusting piece of literature you will ever read. It really is one hundred per cent guaranteed filth.

kurt– (flipping through the pages) Ya . . that's good that's good, but er . . ha ha fifty zousand, Charles . . .

charles– But Kurt, you old war criminal, you really must appreciate what this fabulous obscenity trial has done for Alan's career. I mean we are talking telephone numbers.

kurt– (putting the book down) Oh well, it seems that once again Charles, you have me by ze short penis hairs . . . ok.

    The Zephyr draws up in the background. They all hoot and wave at Charles.

charles– Oh look, there's Alan now...

> He gets up. The waiter appears with the bill and hands it to Charles.

waiter– Your bill, sir.

charles– Thank you. (To Kurt.) We're all settled, are we?

> He puts his hat on and picks up a contract.
>
> You leave this with me . . . (He hands the bill to Kurt). .... and I'll leave this with you.
>
> Charles walks out to the car and gets in. They drive off.

Desmond is pacing up and down his patio. He looks up the road and sees the Zephyr approaching with a dust cloud in the distance. He puts on his dark glasses and cool face and climbs back in the hammock. As the car approaches the house, it slows down and Kix jumps out. The car veers off the road and crashes into Desmond's car. They all climb out, laughing and whooping. Alan, Eleanor, Jeremy and Kix head straight for the front door. Desmond waves coolly at them. They walk into the house without noticing him. Charles, a little way behind, stops to look at the outside of the house. Desmond clears his throat. Charles sees him. Desmond waves.

desmond– Hi.

> Charles looks back at the house.

charles– Beautiful. Very beautiful pad you have. Who handles the insurance?

> Desmond climbs out of the hammock and strolls up to Charles.

desmond– Huh. Who needs it? The world's going to end tomorrow, daddy.

charles– (producing a typed sheet and a pen) Umm. Too true. Just sign this waiver will you – Alan's
dying to meet you.

desmond– Phew . . . Alan . . . It's so weird to think he's in my house....(Desmond signs. Charles starts
walking off.) Smashing up my car. Ha . . . that's really him, isn't it?

> Desmond sees that Charles has disappeared into the house.

In the large kitchen, Kix opens a cupboard and some tins fall out.
Desmond strolls along the corridor. He looks in at the kitchen. Kix has already opened one tin. Down the corridor, Alan is opening the drawing-room door.

desmond– Huh. I like what you did to my car. It was brilliant. Really brilliant.

>Alan puts his head on Desmond's shoulder.

alan– It's going to be a great party, Desmond.

desmond– It's really free, isn't it?

>Alan shuts the door in Desmond's face. Desmond looks at Jeremy, who is on the phone in the hallway. Jeremy glares at him. He goes to the kitchen.

jeremy– Melbourne! Melbourne in Australia! Oh bloody hell!

>He hits the phone.
>Kix is in the kitchen eating out of one of the four tins he has opened. As Desmond walks in he is looking through the fridge.

desmond– Hi. I'm Desmond.

kix– I'm hungry, where do you keep the cream?

desmond– (devastated) Oh cream . . .

>Kix slams the fridge door and picks up some car keys from the table.

kix– These your car keys, Des?

desmond– Er . . . yah.

> Kix walks out the door.
>
> Desmond walks down the corridor. He hears the sound of Eleanor's scat singing coming from the drawing-room. He smiles with satisfaction and opens the drawing-room door.
> Eleanor is sitting cross-legged on the floor scat singing. Alan, wearing sun-glasses, is sitting on the coffee table nodding his head in time. Charles is sitting on the sofa reading through contracts. Desmond saunters over and sits cross-legged at Alan's feet, puts on a pair of sunglasses and begins nodding his head like Alan. After a while Alan starts lightly tapping the coffee table. Desmond quickly jumps up and grabs a pair of bongos off the wall, bringing nail and plaster with them. He sits down and starts feverishly hammering a frenzied beat on the bongos, eyes closed in ecstasy.
> In the corridor Jeremy is shouting on the phone, with one hand over his ear to cover up the din from the bongos.

jeremy– I don't care if you're happily married and you've got four kids and you've emigrated to Australia. Look why can't we forget all that and just start again for God's sake!

> Still playing the bongos, Desmond is waving his head in a frenzy. Eleanor is watching T.V. Alan is on the sofa with his arm around Charles.

charles– And he was sucking and sucking and sucking . . .

> Desmond is playing even louder and shouting.

. . . and he put an ordinary drinking straw into the nick and blew it up to the size of a balloon and said do you want to play pat ball.

> We see Jeremy's hand suddenly snatch the bongos from Desmond's lap and throw them through the window. Smash. Jeremy goes out, slamming the door.

On the beach. In 8mm colour film, the camera wavers across sand and weeds, following a trickle of water. There is the sound of the saxophone. We see a thin torrent of water and pan upwards out of focus.
Back in black and white, we see Anne, a young Canadian film enthusiast on her knees filming the saxophone player pissing into the sand. He has his back to us.

anne– Oh, that's really too much.!

> We pan away from Anne to the front view of the house and the driveway beyond. In the distance we see a milk float coming down the drive.
> Kix is at the wheel of the milk float and is searching around for the brake. Instead he drives into the back of the crashed Zephyr. He gets out and goes to the side of the float and looks for the cream by pulling out a crate of milk which crashes to the ground. He finds the cream and takes one carton, then goes into the house.
> Charles appears on the verandah and looks down the garden. Suddenly he hears Anne's voice.

anne– Hi! You here for the weekend?

> Charles looks around him, then up at the roof and sees Anne with her cine camera.

charles– Er . . .

anne– Me too, but I don't know yet. I mean what's a weekend? It's two days right? I mean are you sleeping with any of these people? I'm sorry can you look at the beach, your bald spot's going to look really great in colour . . . ok ok. No I'm trying to get into underground films but I'm on the roof at the moment. That's a joke. Maybe it's not funny to you I don't know, but it's a free country anyway so what the hell. D'you know Desmond? He seems kinda young but I don't know. I only just met him so I don't know whether I'm sleeping with him but he's got a nice house. I think I'm confused but I don't know.

In the drawing-room Alan, Kix and Eleanor are sitting around on the floor. The sax player is playing in the corner. Desmond comes in carrying a crate of scotch.

kix– (waving his jemmy around) So of course, I bashed his head in . . . and you know what, she called me–(Pointing to Eleanor) a cold-blooded murderer.

He laughs. Eleanor lets out one of her screams and rolls over, her legs in the air.

eleanor– Stop! Stop! It's too crazy, I'm turning into a negro!

alan– Get to the back of the bus.

Desmond puts the scotch on the coffee table.

desmond– Yeah, Yeah, I'm turning into an Italian. (He sticks his foot out.) Look, pointed shoes!

Alan reaches over and pulls out a bottle of scotch.

alan– You remember the Ruler, Kix? That big Negro with a twelve-inch wang.

kix– The one who was stretching underpants for Nureyev – yeah, I remember.

He helps himself to the bottle.

eleanor– Wow!

She takes the bottle.

alan– He was living over a jazz dive near the swamp and er . . .

kix– . . . Walked like a tripod.

Alan takes a swig.

alan– We drove south one day and picked up this strange lesbian . . . dwarf at a roadside motel and she had like this suitcase (Coughs.) full of frogs you know. Maybe I bought a couple, I can't remember. And Joey was being quite weird. I mean he's a great guy and all that but he had like this awful chronic gasoline habit at the time. I mean by the time we reached Marrakesh he was just busting for a gallon.

eleanor– That's so jazz, Alan, go on.

alan– And I was like dying for a cigarette but the man was like a total fire hazard. I mean we'd been close for years, but when he started to . . . you know, glow in the dark, I thought, oh oh it's time to split.

Eleanor lets out a scream.

eleanor– Oh it's so damn crazy when you talk weird, Alan!

desmond– Yeah come on everybody! Let's go crazy apeshit!

He tips over an ashtray.

Charles is seated on the verandah. Anne is filming him from under a table.

anne– You know how I see you? I see you as this weird kinda Fellini business type, you know where you love your wife but you're screwing around cause you're so rich . . . and maybe you're corrupt, I don't know. I mean what exactly do you do for Alan?

charles– I do as little as possible.

Desmond appears on the verandah.

desmond– Look, just go crazy if you want to. You know, take your clothes off, anything!

In the corridor Jeremy is on the phone.

jeremy– Look, if you don't love me Brenda, I'll just kill myself, O.K? . . . Well you're going to be very very very sorry, aren't you . . .?What? . . . Oh, that's very funny, isn't it? . . . Listen, Brenda, I've got a bloody big gun in my hand, O.K? . . . And I'm not afraid to use it!

Kix appears from the drawing room. He looks at Jeremy for a moment. Jeremy is holding two fingers to his own head. He freezes with embarrassment when he sees Kix, and tries to hide his two fingers under a book. Kix strolls up the corridor and goes into the kitchen. Jeremy waits for him to disappear.

jeremy– Look, I'm probably going to die or end up a cripple O.K? . . this is your last chance to say you love me . . . Shut up! O,K . . that's it, Brenda . . . BANG! (He holds the phone away.) Bang! . . . Bang! . . . Keep away everybody . . .! (He makes the sound of a police siren, then puts the phone back to his ear and drops to his knees.) Oh God! Aaargh! The pain! Aargh . . . look what you've done Brenda! Blood! Erk it's all over the floor. Oh God, it's awful. Oh Brenda, I can't stand it . . . everything's going black! . . .

He writhes around on the floor. Kix has reappeared from the kitchen and is at the other end of the corridor trying to prise open the electric meter with his jemmy. Desmond emerges from the drawing room and looks at Jeremy, puzzled.

kix– Pssst . . . Des come here. Look what I've found.

Desmond walks up to Kix, who is panting with exertion. The meter door looks bent and twisted.

desmond– Oh yeah, . . . let's fuse the lights and kiss the girls.

kix– You're crazy, Des. Catch hold of this.

Desmond leans on the jemmy.

Pull!

Kix puts his hand between the wall and the meter. Sparks fly.

desmond– Won't you get a shock?

kix– Only if there's no money.

desmond– Phew! This is a crime isn't it. This is real Genet.

With a sound of grating metal the box opens and the money spills out. Jeremy is sitting with his back to the wall. Knees drawn up, full of quiet remorse.

jeremy– Why don't you love me? Have you found somebody more interesting? I don't understand . . . Is it something I said?

In the drawing-room Alan is sitting cross-legged. Eleanor is doing a handstand against the wall her dress is over her face.

eleanor– Why do I feel so crazy, Alan? I feel like I'm going through a stargate. Maybe it's the diet pills, maybe it's Buddha . . .

alan– Maybe it's that dress, Eleanor, you've been wearing it for an hour.

eleanor– I just want to be happy, Alan. When I get home, you know what I'm going to do? I'm going to leave Simon.

She slides down the walls and crawls across the floor, picks up a bottle of scotch.

I'm going to find myself a really wild jazz guitarist, and shack up in a ghetto. You know, sit around on the porch all day eating ice cream . . . and we'd like have no money, you know really poor, but we wouldn't care.

She gazes into the distance and grabs his knee.

Yes . . . yes . . . Then in the evening we'd take in washing and sing negro spirituals.

alan– Ummm . . . You'll love Shepherd's Bush.

Anne walks in backwards through the french windows filming. She is followed by Charles, who is trying to ignore her.

anne– O.K. You're a successful businessman . . . You're in a hurry . . . You've got some big deal to clinch. Maybe you're impotent, I don't know . . . You hate your wife, O.K. . . .

We cut to Anne's 8mm colour cine film. Charles is a blur. He is trying to avoid her by sitting on the sofa reading a magazine.

charles– My God, you really are a total menace, aren't you?

anne– That's great! You hate publicity, you get so mad when you see a camera.

charles– Look honey, just bugger off, will you?

She moves the camera across the room to Alan, who is still talking to Eleanor.

anne– That's great! You're thinking about murdering your mistress.

alan– Honestly, I really think two legs are a handicap, Eleanor. Just chop it off. I mean at least it's going to make you look very surreal . . . well different anyway.

anne– Just go on talking, Alan.

Alan pulls a face at the camera.

That's good. Now read a poem. You wanna read a poem?

She pans across to Eleanor.

alan– What's my role in this movie?

anne– Anything . . . Anything you like.

eleanor– I'll be a gold-digger.

Anne pans back to Eleanor, who takes some cash from a bag and waves it at the camera.

anne– That's good. You really like money. You try to eat it.

Eleanor licks the money.

O.K. . . . now you go to the businessman. You give him some money.

With a childish pout. Eleanor walks over to Charles.

O.K. . . . . You, business guy – grab the money from her.

Charles is looking through contracts. He takes the money without looking up...

Yeah, great! smile at the camera, like you're really pleased you ripped her off. Here, smoke this cigar.

She hands him a cigar.

Now have an orgy. Come on everybody, do something really gross. Like pretend it's a dinner party.

Kix is half under the kitchen sink, levering at the lead pipes. Desmond is standing watching him.

kix– You see lead is very valuable, Des, because it's heavy. You see the heavier something is, the more valuable it is. Of course, the only real exception to this rule is concrete. On the other hand, diamonds are expensive.

    Kix gives a final wrench on the pipes. There is a sound of water escaping.

In the drawing room Anne pans round and picks out Eleanor, who is switching on the T.V.

anne– O.K., Eleanor. Now you're a simple nowhere housewife, you've got ten kids and menstrual prolems.

    Eleanor pulls a face.

eleanor– What am I doing?

anne– You're naked and you're watching T.V. . . . . a game show.

eleanor– O.K. I'm really bored.

    Eleanor tries to look really bored.

anne– Yeah, yeah, terrific. Now, here comes your homosexual junkie son to rape you.

eleanor– Why should he do that?

anne– Why does a homosexual junkie son do anything?

    End of 8mm film sequence.

Desmond and Kix are in the attic. Kix (soaking wet) is trying to lever open a cupboard.

kix– What's your old man keep in here, Des?

desmond– Oh that's his gun cupboard.

kix– (levering harder) Oh triffic. Where's the nearest post office?

Kix and Desmond are seen walking out of the house. Kix has an armful of rifles.

desmond– I guess you live for the moment. huh?

kix– I am at the moment, yeah.

    They disappear from view.

    We hear the sound of Eleanor singing and playing a guitar. The light begins to fade on the house.

Eleanor is singing a cacky folk song and strumming a guitar, by candlelight. Alan is playing the bongos and Desmond is on Kazoo. The others are asleep on the floor.

View of the sand dunes and sea in the early morning. The sax player is strolling along the beach playing. Front view of the house in early morning. Sound of saxophone and cock crowing. Desmond, Alan, Eleanor, Anne and Kix are all asleep in sleeping bags on the drawing room floor. The room is bathed in sunshine. The drawing-room door suddenly bursts open and Jeremy strides in.

jeremy– All sleeping well, are you?!

> He goes out slamming the door. Pause. He re-enters.

Just carry on, O.K.? Sleep! The stupid bomb's only just around the corner, for God's sake.

> He walks up and down.

Doesn't anybody care around here? Go on, sleep. Go on sleeping.

> Nobody stirs. He goes to the window. Pause.

Bang! Bang! Radiation! Fall out everywhere! Oh wow, it's the holocaust, man. Come on everybody, let's smoke a reefer. Let's take our stupid clothes off and meditate.

> No reaction.

Oh what's the bloody point?

> He points at the ceiling.

Stop bomb, stop! Alan wants to write a poem about you.

> He goes out, slamming the door and immediately re-enters, carrying a paint-pot and brush.

It's all right! There's only a million corpses in the kitchen.

> He goes out through french windows to garden. He begins furiously painting the lawn black. Anne appears through the french windows, in her nightdress, smoking a cigarette. Her cine camera is under her arm.

anne– Wow! That's crazy. What are you doing, Jeremy?

jeremy– It's pretty obvious, isn't it?

> She stands for a moment, watching him paint the grass.

anne– Look, I know this may sound really crass, Jeremy, but I like you.

> She walks nearer to him.

I like your style. I like your naked aggression. I really like the way you don't sleep at night.

jeremy– People think it's easy to be a rebel. Well it bloody isn't. They just write stupid plays about me.

. . . it makes me so mad.

> He goes on painting the lawn. Anne looks through the camera.

anne– Oh wow . . . that's really beautiful.

jeremy– We're all in the Garden of Death.

> He looks up.

Death and silence everywhere.

anne– Paint the garden . . . it really looks good.

jeremy– I feel there's a black wall (He starts painting a circle round himself.) . . . . It's surrounding me . . . I'm a prisoner . . . a prisoner of Brenda.

anne– O.K. so! You're a rebel *and* a prisoner.

> He sits in the circle.

You're an enigma. Who are you?

jeremy (staring into the distance) My name's Jeremy.

anne– O.K. What are you thinking, Jeremy?

jeremy– I'm thinking about . . . (He looks at the cornfield across road.) About cornfields.

anne– A yellow cornfield.

jeremy– Black . . . Yes, it's very black.

anne– You're painting it?

jeremy– No, I've set fire to it.

anne– Oh beautiful. What are you doing now?

jeremy– I'm watching a funeral. It's me . . . I'm being buried . . . Oh no . . . wet earth and darkness.

anne– That's a bitch of a nightmare, isn't it?

> He looks around him.

jeremy– Oh look . . . there's a tunnel! It's black . . . no, leave me! I want to stay . . . I didn't ask to be born. I don't want war . . . Oh, what's the bloody point?

anne– Oh, that's crazy, The birth of a rebel. I'm here, Jeremy.

jeremy– Oh look over there – deprived childhood. Don't hit me again, Mummy. No, not the broom cupboard, Daddy . . . Ouch, ouch . . . growing pains and teenage violence. Oh no, sand in my face . . . She's laughing at me She's breaking my heart. He's breaking my nose.

anne– Is it Brenda?

jeremy– Yes, Yes. Look out everybody . . . teenage suicide. . . .

> He starts slashing at his wrists with the paintbrush, then bursts into tears.

It's all so bloody futile.

> Anne puts down her camera, stubs out her cigarette and goes down on her knees to comfort Jeremy. Pause.

anne– Jeremy . . . do you . . . love Brenda?

jeremy– Love's stupid, O.K.?

anne– But, Jeremy . . .

jeremy– Look . . .(He wipes his eyes.) Supposing I say 'I love you', O.K.?

anne– Yeah!

jeremy– And supposing we're both drowning at sea and I can't save you because I can't swim . . . That's not love, for God's sake.

anne– Oh come on, that's not your fault, Jeremy.

jeremy– Yes it is! Don't you understand? If I can't save you, that means I don't love you . . . because I really *can* swim.

anne– I don't understand, You just said you couldn't.

jeremy– Bloody hell! Look, it's very simple, O.K?

> He picks up the paintbrush

What's this?

anne– A paintbrush?

jeremy– No!! . . . This is getting so futile!

anne– O.K. It's a symbol. . . .

jeremy– Yes! now do you understand?

Charles is staying in a small bedroom. He puts on his dressing gown and slippers, picks up his attaché case and goes to the bathroom down the corridor.
Eleanor is sitting on the toilet, tearing off strips of paper. Charles hovers in the doorway.

charles– Hi.

eleanor– Come in, Charles. I want to talk to you.

> Charles enters.

I really want to talk to you, Charles.

charles– Sure.

> He shuts the door, opens his attaché case.

eleanor– It's about Alan. I think I love him, but . . . am I too square? I mean Kix is a sweet boy, but Alan . . . Well, he's so famous.

charles– I know.

eleanor– I'd do anything for Alan. It's this leg business, Charles . . . It's so confusing. I mean, where does one get it done?

> She rests her head on her knees

And Simon's going to kill me. I just know it. He's going to beat me black and blue all over. Honestly, Charles, he's such a bastard. You wouldn't believe how possessive he is, and he's so fucking rude to my lovers. . . .

charles– (holding a syringe up to the light) Yes, yes it is a problem, isn't it?

The kitchen door is half open. There is a scrabbling sound from behind the door. Desmond appears in the doorway in his pyjamas. He is trying to find the plastic toy in a cereal packet. He looks up and down the corridor then disappears into the kitchen.

eleanor– (still in the bathroom) I really don't care what Simon thinks. I don't know why I go on about him . . . It's Alan. Alan's right, two legs are dull. They're so boring, so middle-class and deep down I've always know it . . . I can't think what it is, Charles, that's held me back for so long . . . Is it fear? Is it prejudice? Is it superstition? What is it?

> Charles is closing his case.

charles– Umm . . . well. I've enjoyed our little chat, Eleanor . . .

> He smiles and walks out.

In the kitchen Desmond pours out the cereal into a bowl, then hides the packet in a cupboard. He sits at the table, pours some milk over the cereal and takes a furtive spoonful. He gets up and picks up a book and opens it at random.

desmond– Hey crazy baby this – (He looks at the cover.) **Hey crazy baby this Orlofs** – (He looks at the cover again.) . . . **this Orlofsky's an out of sight cat.** (With confidence.) **Hey crazy baby, this Orlofsky's an out of sight cat.**

> He takes another spoonful of cereal and freezes as he hears footsteps on the stairs. He looks at the table and sees that the toast is in a silver toast rack. He shakes out the toast and arranges it in a rough pile on the table, then quickly pours a few spots of milk on the table.
> We see Charles reaching the bottom of the stairs.
> Desmond is intently reading his book. Sound of footsteps approaching.

desmond– **Hey crazy baby. This Orlofs . . . ker's an out of sight cat.**

> The footsteps go past. He sighs and puts down the book. Suddenly the kitchen door opens and Alan walks on followed by Kix in his Y-Fronts and a raincoat.

kix– Well you do that, Alan, and I'll cut your ears off.

alan– My God, you really are a doughnut Kix. How are you Desmond?

kix– Watcha, Des.

> As Desmond puts another spoonful of cereal in his mouth. Kix goes up to him and embraces him, crushing Desmond's head against his chest. Desmond chokes, and showers "Coco pops" over the table. Kix searches through the cupboards for the "Coco pops". He finds them and starts digging around for the plastic toy. Alan picks up the book.

alan– Ummm. (He flips through the pages.) **Why, Desmond, you really are quite a booksnake, aren't you?**

desmond– Some people think Orlofsky's pretty weird, but I think he's really sincere, don't you?

alan– Well of course he's a total phoney, and a complete literary fraud. (He butters some toast.) The man was an absolute mess when I knew him. You know, like, his rectum was completely burnt out with Yage abuse . . .

> Kix empties the entire packet of "Coco pops" over the table.

. . . . Terrible trots, just terrible. He had, like, these enormous brown . . .

kix– Hang on . . . who's had the submarine?

In the corridor Charles is on the phone. His voice is booming down the corridor.

charles– Jack . . . How are you? . . . I'm sorry to hear about the liver . . . Pardon? . . . What? . . . I can't hear you . . . There's a terrible rattle on this line . . . Oh, it's your lungs . . . Well listen, I know you're in dreadful pain so I'll keep it short . . . Now, I've got your medical bill here . . . do you really need all those drugs? . . . Yes, I know you're dying, Jack. That's why I queried it. . . .

Jeremy is standing in the sea, up to his waist, fully clothed. Anne is filming him from the water's edge.

anne– O.K., what you're trying to tell me is that nobody understands you, right? They treat you like an alien and they want to put you in a zoo, is that it?

jeremy– (looking out to sea) Nobody understands me . . . . They think I'm just joking.

Anne wades into the sea, also fully clothed and puts her head on his shoulder.

anne– I understand you, Jeremy.

Jeremy and Anne are sitting nose to nose on a sand dune. Pause. . .

anne– I think you're a very attractive and very angry young man.

jeremy– Well, I'm pretty fierce, O.K?

Long pause.

anne– Jeremy . . . are those teeth capped?

Jeremy is standing in the hollow of a sand dune. Anne is sitting cross-legged on the side of the dune.

jeremy– . . . Huh! They say there goes good old Jeremy, he's a pretty easy-going guy. Let's have a crazy free time. You know, come on Jeremy, let's stay up all night and smoke cigarettes . . . Pause. . . Huh! It's so bloody easy, isn't it. But they don't know. They don't know the real me. I mean underneath, I'm pretty serious.

Anne and Jeremy are walking on the seashore.

jeremy– . . . they call you an artist, but they don't want to know, in case you try to break their system, in case you tell the truth. It's all a stupid conspiracy . . .

> They stop. Anne puts on some Lipsol.

They say be a communist homosexual, Jeremy! and things like that, just on and on and on until . . . I don't know just . . . Oh, what's the bloody point . . .?

> Anne looks at Jeremy.

anne– Jeremy, do you want to kiss me?

jeremy– (looks around furtively) Where?

Anne and Jeremy are standing behind a bush in the garden he is kissing her with his mouth closed; they both have wet faces and spit running off their chins.

jeremy– Phew, you're pretty good at snogging. (Anne wipes his face with a handkerchief.) Look, I know this is a bit sudden, but let's get engaged, because I think I love you, O.K.?

anne– Cut.

Front view of the house. Sound of saxophone.

Alan, Desmond, Eleanor and Kix are lying around in the drawing-room. Alan is tapping the bongos and eating chocolates. Desmond is cross-legged swaying to the rhythm. Eleanor is lying arms outstretched and Kix is trying to open a toilet slot machine with his jemmy.

kix– And there was Curly bleeding from the neck, so I thought I know what I'll do, I'll stick on a tourniquet. And of course when I came back I couldn't believe it. His face was completely black and his hair had gone like dead straight. I thought that's really amazing, he looks just like Chuck Berry.

desmond– Yeah rhythm and blues. Crazy man!

kix– no but the funny thing was, there was this strange sort of unearthly smell, bit like Maltesers. And you know what, everytime I eat Maltesers . . .

eleanor– . . . You think of Curly.

kix– . . . Yeah.

alan– All my friends taste like diet pills.

eleanor– What do I taste like, Kix?

kix– Valium.

      Eleanor puts her hand in Kix's shirt and whispers in his ear.

alan– Ya ya, I remember when Sidney died of sodomy in Singapore. We had to bury him in the wardrobe . . .

eleanor– Come on, Kix, let's do it. I want to do it.

      Kix gets up as Charles walks in.

alan– . . . We were at the Hilton Hotel overlooking the Turkish baths . . . Room 401 . . .

kix– Just lend me your suit and passport for a few hours, that's all I'm asking, Charles.

alan– It was, like, really terrible terrible service. But you know me . . . (He looks hard at Desmond.) I'm just a blob of rancid butter when it comes to brown boys in sarongs.

desmond– (shifting uneasily) Actually, I'm buddhist.

charles– Why must you always involve me, Kix?

kix– Because I love you, man.

charles– I love you too, Kix.

      Desmond has edged himself closer to Eleanor. With a fake yawn he puts his arm behind her head, and whispers in her ear.

desmond– I want to do it to you.

eleanor– (loudly) What?

desmond– I want to do it to you.

kix– I've got to have it, Charles, I've got to have it. It's jazz, Charles. It's Charlie Parker, it's . . .

charles– Out of the question.

eleanor– (louder) I can't hear what you're saying, Desmond. Speak up.

desmond– Nothing.

eleanor– No, what did you say, Desmond?

desmond– (even quieter) I want to do it to you.

eleanor– You want to do it to me? You want to do what to me? What do you mean you want to do it to me?

desmond– It.

eleanor– It! You want to do *it* to me? Listen everybody! Desmond wants to do it to me!

Front view of the house. Charles is sitting on the verandah with a bottle of scotch and a Micky Spillane book. Desmond appears from the french window.

desmond– Pretty free here, isn't it?

charles– (pouring another whisky) Well , I'm not paying.

      Desmond sits noisily next to Charles.

desmond– Yes it's really going well. Everybody's having a pretty groovy time. I don't suppose it's really your scene, is it? I mean, you're pretty much the odd man out around here.

charles– Oh I don't know . . . free scotch, no phone bill. I find it quite relaxing, really.

      Charles takes off his wig and starts combing it.

desmond– I guess you're really into money and business and being straight, aren't you? I mean, I don't know what you're doing here, you know . . .cause we're all crazy poets . . . I mean phew! I just don't care about anything. I'm absolutely coasting. I feel very cheese. Yes, very very cheese

. . .cause I'm a poet, you know.

      He produces a wad of papers.

Would you like to see my poems?

      He hands one to Charles.

This one I wrote years ago . . .

Anne is alone in the drawing room. Her camera is on a tripod. She stands in front of it, musses her hair, rips her shirt, then switches on the camera.

anne– Rape.

> She throws herself on the sofa.

On the verandah Desmond hands another sheet to Charles.

desmond– . . . It's not very good but . . .

charles– Yes, it's embarrassing, isn't it?

> He puts the sheet down. Desmond hands him another one.

desmond– This one's about my first trauma. My girl friend was just back from boarding school, when her pony Bimbo died.

> Sound of gunshot.

Close shot of two pottery ducks on a wall being shot to pieces. Kix is sitting by the kitchen table. He reloads the shotgun. Eleanor is washing her bra and knickers in the kitchen sink.

eleanor– I had a really crazy time at school. I was laying the teachers and just getting into everything that was going . . . all the girls hated me, they were so jealous.

Desmond hands Charles another poem.

desmond– And this one's all about tedium and drudgery.

charles– (handing it straight back) My God, yes.

Eleanor hangs up the washing on a rail. Kix fires at two small plates as they pop out of the toaster. They shatter over the kitchen. Desmond pops his head round the door. He smiles awkwardly.

desmond– How's dinner going?

kix– (reloading the gun) Dinner! That's a good idea! (He gets up.) What do you fancy, Des? Duck? Pig? Horse?

> He goes out. Desmond strolls around the kitchen.

desmond– Look. I think maybe you've got the wrong idea about me, Eleanor. You know . . . I'm not a virgin, O.K.? I've slept around quite a bit you know and er. . .

eleanor– Well, you've certainly got the wrong idea about *me,* Desmond. I may be a very sensuous woman but I'm not a common nymphomaniac, O.K?

She hangs up some soaking panties.

desmond– Oh come on, you must like me a bit. You wouldn't be staying here otherwise.

eleanor– My God, you're such a drip. You really can't help yourself, can you? What is it about me that makes men do this?

desmond– Well, it's natural isn't it? If a woman's attractive?

eleanor– What about that other girl . . . Anne. She's attractive, isn't she? I mean, if you just want a woman's body, why don't you ask her?

desmond– It's you I want . . . is that so bad?

eleanor– Oh, I see. It's me, is it? Jesus! Next you'll be saying you're in love with me or something gooey!

desmond– No, all I said . . .

eleanor– So it's just my body, isn't it?

desmond– Yes . . . No . . .

eleanor– Look, if you want my body, you can have it, only don't come whining to me afterwards.

Kix is seen strolling up the driveway, shooting at everything he sees.

Desmond is in bed with Eleanor. He is trying to kiss her passionately. She is ignoring him and reading a car manual. Alan is sitting on the bed eating chocolates. There is the sound of gunshots in the background.

alan– I don't think this sex thing is happening, Desmond. Eleanor looks bored.

desmond– Is she?

alan– Eleanor . . .

eleanor– (putting her book down) What?

alan– When Desmond is doing that to you, does the earth move at all?

eleanor– No. Only the bed.

        She picks up her book.

alan– Ummm. (Eats another chocolate.) Maybe I can think of something . . . Yes, let's try it this way. Forget about Desmond.

desmond– Eh?

eleanor– Great! Go on.

alan– You're in um . . . You're in Cairo. You're in the maternity ward at the Cairo General. There's disease everywhere – typhoid, leprosy . . .

eleanor– . . . malaria, dysentry . . .

desmond– . . . Measles.

Anne is lying on the sofa in the drawing room, smoking an after-sex cigarette. Jeremy is pacing round the room.

jeremy– That was pretty amazing. I didn't think I could do it like that, you know – just like shaking hands. I mean, I haven't even met your parents. It's so casual.

anne– What the hell do my parents have to do with it?

jeremy– O.K., maybe I'm square. But you know, I don't usually just do it with somebody on a first date, O.K?

anne– Oh that really makes me feel good.

jeremy– Look. I don't know about you, Anne. I don't know *anything* about you.

anne– Such as?

jeremy– Well, things like . . . where you were born . . . whether you like table tennis . . . how many 'O'levels you've got . . . whether you like Cliff Richard. I don't know . . .

Eleanor and Desmond are still in bed. Alan is now between them.

eleanor– Oh wow! That's so absolutely damn crazy Alan!

alan– Of course he was much younger then, my dears. But I remember one time Charles going to bed with a koala bear. A virgin . . . although he didn't know it at the time. She was a sweet little thing . . . do anything for a banana.

    Sound of a car crashing.

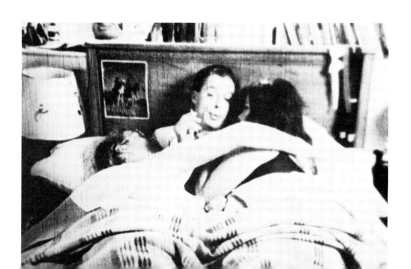

Kix has turned up in another car and crashed it into the back of the milk float. He and two young girls, Judy and Tracy, get out, giggling. Kix is carrying a crate of booze. The two girls inspect the damage.

tracy– You've really gone and dented it.

judy– Yeah . . . you've damaged it.

kix– (he starts walking to the house) I can start cars, but I can't stop them.

      The girls follow. Judy puts her finger to her head and does a 'he's mad' gesture. They giggle.

Front view of the house. The evening light is fading. In the house, lights are on. There is the sound of a party in full swing.

In the drawing room Kix and Anne are playing bongos. Eleanor is scat singing. Jeremy is dancing. Alan is drinking. Desmond is swigging from a bottle and swaying about. Charles is tapping his fingers on his attaché case and the two girls are sitting primly on the edge of the sofa, looking bemused. All except Charles and the two girls are dressed in party clothes. Desmond lurches over towards Tracy and Judy.

desmond– Listen, if you want to break something – it's O.K. with me.

      Judy does her 'he's mad' gesture. Desmond staggers across the room and starts dancing with Jeremy who immediately sits down. Eleanor has draped herself seductively over Charles.

charles– Cigarette?

eleanor– I like to smoke *after*, thank you, darling

charles– Umm . . . I like to smoke instead.

      Desmond leaps around and falls backwards over a coffee table. Kix is talking to Judy and Tracy.

kix– Having a good time?

judy– It's all right.

      Tracy blows a bubble.

kix– How old are you?

judy– Fourteen.

kix– Oh, got any younger sisters?

      She shakes her head 'no'.

  Or pets?

Eleanor breathing in Charles' ear

eleanor– Oh Charles, you're so callous. It really turns me on.

charles– I find the thought of it quite vile.

eleanor– Oh yes, come on be mean to me Charles, be mean.

charles– I'm not trying to be sexy, Eleanor. I really do despise you.

Tracy whispers to Judy. They giggle.

judy– Who's he?

Pointing at Jeremy.

kix– He's Jeremy.

They both giggle. Jeremy gives a cool smile.
Fancy him, do you?

tracy– Might do . . .

kix– Jeremy!

Jeremy pretends not to hear.

tracy– Don't do that . . .

kix– (louder) Jeremy!

Jeremy reluctantly looks up. Kix winks and points repeatedly at the two girls. Behind him the two girls are shaking their heads and doing their 'he's mad' gesture. Eleanor comes over and crouches in front of Kix and the two girls.

eleanor– Hello! Who are you?

kix– This is Judy and this is Tracy.

eleanor– They're so pretty aren't they . . . and so clean. I think girls of thirteen look so sexy, don't you? Are you both virgins?

Alan staggers over to Charles, who is avidly reading a record cover.

alan– Come on, Charles. Give us a kiss, you old closet clerk.

charles– (looking at his watch) My God, is it ten o'clock already?

alan– Oh come on, Charles. Let's strip off, like we did in the old days. Show em that funny muscle.

charles– (getting up) I'll see you in the morning, Alan.

Charles walks out. Alan falls over. Anne sits beside him.

alan– That's Charles. He's an unbelievable shit. I've always hated him . . . (Breaking down.) Isn't he fantastic.

Anne sits down, cross legged, beside him.

anne– Hi, I've been wanting to sit down and have a real natter with you the whole weekend but er . . . you always seemed like to have a lot on your mind and everything.

alan– Who the hell are you?

anne– I'm working on a project. It's a film about these two pygmies who run away from home and make it big in show business. . . . You know, and it sets out to show the problems they have breaking into Hollywood. It's really about pygmy alienation in the twentieth century. The main character is a sort of short, black James Dean and, as you can imagine, nothing goes right for him.

The door swings open. Desmond enters with his face blacked up, carrying an electric guitar.

desmond– Modern jazz everbody! Let's go!

He plugs his guitar direct into the mains and gets electrocuted. They all clap and cheer with cries of "Go it Sooty". He starts twitching. They change the bongo rhythm to be in time with his convulsions.

Charles is in bed, peeling a banana, holding it upright and throwing a phallic shadow on the wall.

Downstairs Desmond is doing a Chuck Berry duck walk with his guitar. Anne is filming the party with her cine camera gaffer-taped to her head. We see a short 8mm sequence of the party from weird positions and spinning round. In one corner Judy and Tracy are chatting up Jeremy. Alan is talking to Eleanor.

alan– And Charles at the time was married to this woman in Hong Kong. She was a suma wrestler who like did a spot of whoring on the side. Her speciality was like . . . breaking your arm at the height of orgasm. Four visits was enough for anybody.

tracy– Do you know these people, then?

judy– Yeah, are they friends of yours, Jeremy?

jeremy– Not friends really. Just people I know.

tracy– They're really stupid, aren't they?

judy– And old.

> Desmond who has been jumping about with his guitar, falls into the fire. Everybody claps and cheers. He emerges in flames. Anne films him. Kix finds a fire extinguisher and turns it on Desmond.

anne– Not yet. I'm out of focus.

> Kix puts out the flames

O.K. that's beautiful.

kix– That was brilliant, Des.

desmond– Come on everybody. Let's go crazy bloody apeshit.

> He goes and kicks in the television. They cheer and clap. He starts climbing the curtains and pulls them down.

Charles is in bed crushing the banana and rubbing the pulp into his hands.

charles– Oh dear . . . oh dear . . . oh dear.

Downstairs.

judy– Not much of a party, is it?

> Desmond picks up a picture and smashes it. Kix hands him a vase.

kix– Here you are, Des.

> Desmond chucks it through the window.
> Front view of the house at night. Sound of breaking glass and cheering. Fade out.

Same view in the early morning.

Desmond is asleep in the bottom drawer of a wardrobe with his feet sticking out. Anne and Jeremy are crashed out amongst the debris. Kix and Alan are quietly talking and smoking.

There is a clumping scraping sound from the corridor. The door opens and Eleanor enters on crutches. She has a leg missing. Pause.

eleanor– Alan . . . Alan look I did it . . .I finally cut it off.

     Pause

alan– Where's the leg?

eleanor– At the hospital.

     Pause.

alan– But it's the leg we're interested in . . .

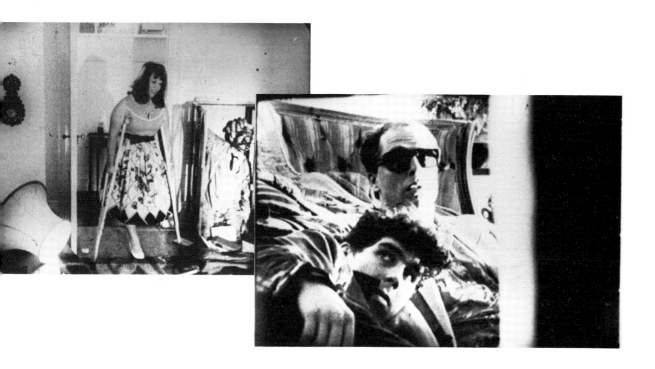

We see the beach, the sea and the garden in the foreground. Sound of the saxophone. Saxophone player comes into view in the distance. He walks slowly along the sea shore playing. Sound of gunshot. The sax player falls over.

Freeze.

Written by Peter Richardson and Peter Richens

CAST		jeremy	Rik Mayall	kurt	Robbie Coltrane
desmond	Adrian Edmondson	kix	Danny Peacock	judy	Zoe Clarke
alan	Peter Richardson	anne	Jennifer Saunders	tracy	Kim Pappas
eleanor	Dawn French	charles	Nigel Planer	Directed by Bob Spiers	

● **A sweeping panoramic shot of the City of London as dawn rises, set against one of the band's songs, and intercut with shots of individual members of the band playing on stage.**

One two three four five six seven . . . . .
Bad news! Bad news! Bad news!
For you and you and you and you and you,
Bad news! Bad news! Bad news!
For you and you and you and you and you.

Can't you see – devil woman,
Can't you hear – black leather,
Can't you see – screaming vengeance,
Don't you know – bloodlust paranoid metal.

Bad News!
Bad News!
Bad News!

For you and you and you and you
And you,.
Bad News!
Bad News!
Bad News!

The sweeping panoramic shot comes to rest on a block of flats. The camera zooms in on the only window with a light on in the room behind it.
The camera pulls out from a close-up shot of a tape recorder whose dials pulsate to the music we can hear, to reveal the kitchen in Vim's flat. Vim is standing by the cooker with an egg in his hand.

Vim: Ready?
There is a muffled grunt to the affirmative. Vim crack the egg with one hand. He gets egg all over hand. We then hear the voice of the director, Sandy.

Sandy's Voice: What's that playing on the tape Vim?

For you and you and you
and you and you.

Can't you see
Heavy Rainbow,
Can't you hear
Twisted tiger,
Can't you see
Hair on fire,
Don't you know
Demon battleaxe steel.

Vim: It's a tape *(he laughs at his own joke)*. No, it's our latest song actually. Yeah. Its called 'Bad News'. Although you've probably worked that out, it's a sort of statement.

Sandy's Voice: A statement on what?

Vim: A statement on . . . look I'll tell you later, right? I only just got up. It's six o'clock in the morning and you're expecting me to blow you minds. Listen to the lyrics.

Sandy's Voice: Pardon?

Vim: The lyrics. Listen to the lyrics.

Vim turns the volume up, just in time for the instrumental to begin.

Sandy's Voice: What sort of feeling have you got about the tour?

Vim: What?

Sandy's Voice: What do you feel about the tour?

Vim: Tour?

Sandy's Voice: Yes.

Vim: Yeah, we're going on tour.

There is a faint sound of someone knocking on the door, but the volume of the music almost drowns it out.

Sandy's Voice: I think there's someone at the door.

Vim: What?

Sandy's Voice: There somebody at the door.

Vim: No, we've got a toilet.

Sandy's Voice: No! The door! There's somebody at the door!

Vim: Oh right.

He fights his way past the camera crew into the hall. The camera follows him.

Vim: Well why doesn't someone bloody well answer it? You're all standing there.

Vim turns the corner in the corridor, the camera picks up on the pictures of women, skulls, and motorbikes that adorn the walls, we hear Vim answering the door.

Neighbour: Do you known what time it is?

Vim: It's about six innit? Has anyone got the right time?

Neighbour: It's five past six.

The camera rounds the corner and we see the neighbour in his pyjama trousers, vest and dressing gown.

Neighbour: Now if you don't turn that racket off I shall definitely inform the police.

Vim turns to the camera crew and shouts.

Vim: Look could somebody turn the tape recorder off, you have to unplug it 'cause the button doesn't work. Look I'm sorry mate . . .

Neighbour: Now look son, I've warned you before . . .

The neighbour suddenly clocks the camera. The camera tries to hide but gives up and moves closer to the front door.

What's going on in there? What are you doing?

Vim: Oh it's all right, mate. They're making a film about me. I'm going to be on the telly.

Neighbour: Tell them to turn that camera off.

Vim: Heh?

> *The neighbour stumbles backwards followed by the camera, Vim is edged out of the way. The neighbour hides beind the glass partition on the landing.*

Neighbour: I refuse to be filmed.

> *The camera moves round to the neighbour's side of the partition, the neighbour retreats into the doorway of the lift.*

Neighbour: Turn that thing off!

> *In exasperation the neighbour moves towards the camera and covers the lens with his hands.*

Neighbour: What the bloody hell do you think you're playing at?!

● **Vim is climbing a long flight of stairs in what is obviously a council estate.**

Vim's Voice: I could play 'Stairway to Heaven' when I was twelve.

> *He trips on the stairs and falls out of sight behind the wall. He re-emerges a lot further up the stairs.*

Jimmy Page didn't write it until he was twenty-two.

> *Cut to shot of Vim knocking on a door.*

I think that says quite a lot.

> *The door is opened by Den.*

Den: Did they get it this time?

Vim: What?

Den: I mean did they get another hair in their gate or what?

Vim *(under his breath):* Shut up Den.

Den: Heh?

Vim: Shut up. Oh Christ. *(He turns to the director who is out of shot.)* Look, shall we go again?

Sandy's Voice: No, go with this one.

Vim: But it's crap.

Sandy's Voice: We can cut the beginning off.

> *Den taps his radio microphone.*

Den: Is this mike working? Hello. Hello. One, two, one two.

Sandy's Voice: Yes, Den it's working, it's working. Look we're wasting a lot of film here.

Vim: O.K., O.K., Keep cool. You ready, Den?

Den: What?

Vim: Oh god! Come on!

Den: I'm ready. I'm ready.

Vim: Well get back inside then.

> *Vim pushes Den back inside the door.*

Sandy's Voice: Look, let's go over the other side, Oliver.

> *The camera moves to the other side of the front door, and in doing so reveals the whole camera crew who struggle to get round to the other side and behind the camera.*

Sandy's Voice: O.K.

> *Vim knocks on the door again. Den answers.*

Vim: Hello Den.

Den: Hello Alan.

> *Pause.*

Vim: Vim.

Den: What?

Vim: Vim, Vim. My name is Vim, remember?

Den: Oh yeah, right, sorry, sorry. Er, hello Vim.

Vim: Hello Den. Got your stuff ready then?

Den: Yeah, it's right here in the hall.

Vim: Well come on, we've got to pick up the others yet.

Den: All right Alan. Sorry. Sorry. All right Vim. Vim.

> *Den turns back into the hallway to collect his gear. He talks softly, unaware of the microphone.*

Den: Right, I'm off now mum, bye.

> *He closes the door and walks off after Vim.*

Vim's Voice: Den used to be in this group called 'The Hounds Of Zaroff'. They were rubbish, right, but all you had to do to join was drink half a bottle of vodka and keep it down. He tried six times before he got in.

● **The camera is in the back of the Band's van, looking forward past Vim, who is in the driving seat, and Den, in the passenger's seat. We can see Colin waiting by the side of the road further along.**

Vim: There he is. He's standing outside so you don't see how posh his house is.

> *The van comes to a stop beside Colin.*

Den: Hi Colin.

Colin: Hi Den.

> *Colin moves to the back of the van and gets in the back door.*

Vim's Voice: The only thing that's wrong with Colin is that he can't really play.

Vim: How's it going with you mate? All right?

Colin: Yeah, I feel a bit wrecked actually . . . Bloody hell, it's a bit cramped in here isn't it?

> *Colin clambers over the sound equipment and various members of the film crew to get to the sofa which is jammed up behind the front seats. He sits down.*

Colin: Yeah, I feel a bit wrecked, you know.

Den: Did you see the Whistle Test last night?

Colin: Sort of, yeah. But I . . . . I was really stoned you know, and I drank a bottle of brandy. Yeah, I was with this chick, and we were just about to get down to it when I put my foot through the television set. So it sort of blew up a bit, and set fire to the curtains, and er, I missed the second half of the show.

Den: I bet you mum was really angry.

Colin: She wasn't there, was she Den?

Den: Yeah, but when she gets back.

Colin: No, Den, Den she won't be getting back.

Den: How come?

Colin: 'Cause she's dead.

Den: Heh?

Vim: She's dead, Den.

Den: Oh I get it. So Alan is called Vim, and your mum's dead . . . . Oh no . . . *(He turns to the camera.)* Can we cut this bit as well?

● **Vim is leaning on the doorbell outside Spider's house.**

Vim: Where is he?

Den: Which one's his bedroom do you think?

> *Vim shouts through the letterbox.*

Vim: Come on Spider!

> *Spider opens the door at exactly the same time as Den throws a stone through his bedroom window.*

Spider: What time do you call this then?

Den: I think I've smashed you window Spider, sorry.

> *Spider looks up at the window in question.*

Sorry.

Spider: Never mind Den, it's all anarchy, isn't it?

> *He smiles at the camera.*

Vim: You ready then?

Spider: No, sorry, I've got to go and sign on at half ten.

Vim: What?

Spider: Joke, geddit?

Vim: Very funny.

> *A girl appears behind Spider in the doorway with Spider's bag.*

Girl: Here's your bag, Spider.

Spider: Hey baby, you're my bag!

Girl: Oh Spider!

> *She flings her arms around his neck. Spider moves her back down the hall a little way.*

Spider *(thinking he is out of earshot):* Cry like I told you to or you won't get paid.

> *They move back to the door. The girl bursts into tears and clings to him.*

Girl: Oh no Spider, don't leave me Spider, not now.

> *Spider turns to the camera and smiles.*

Spider: Huh, chicks. See you doll.

> *Spider walks out of shot. The girl stands in the doorway looking directly into camera and waving.*

Vim's Voice: Spider used to have this really big drug problem . . . he couldn't get enough.
Sandy's Voice: Shut the door.

The girl shuts the door hesitantly.

Vim's Voice: That's probably why he's like he is, you know, completely crazed.

Shot of the band in the van. Vim tries to start the engine. The engine sounds completely dead. After three attempts he gives up.
Cut to shot of Colin, Den and Spider pushing the van.

Vim's Voice: But he's a bloody good drummer, though, you know. When I auditioned him he did a forty-six minute drum solo. I mean he would have done a lot more but I can't stand drum solos.

The band manage to bump start the van. Spider and Colin stop pushing but Den runs on after the van.
We cut to the other end of the street, the van comes round the corner having obviously been round the block.

Vim's Voice: Um, life on the road is a lot more interesting than working in a factory. You do a lot more driving around for a start. You always feel as if you're going somewhere, you know?

Colin and Spider get into the van. Den comes running round the corner, knackered, the van sets off, Den runs along behind, trying to catch up.

Den: You tossers!
Spider: See you in Grantham, Den!

● **Cut to shot from inside the van looking out through the front past Spider, Colin and Vim in the driving seat. They pass a couple of girls in school uniform.**

Spider: Hey girls! Slow down, slow down.

The van slows to a halt.

Spider *(out of the window to the girls):* Hey, I like the gear, really kinky!
Cheryl: Don't talk to him Trace, he looks dirty.

Spider: Hey, listen!

Tracey: You making a film then?

Cheryl: Trace!

Spider: Yeah. I'm a rock star.

Tracey: What? You an actor?

Spider: No, rock star. Bad News on the road.

Tracey: Oh, with a band.

Spider: Yeah, can't you read?

Cheryl: Look come on Trace, we're going to be late. Never heard of them anyway.

Spider: Listen, I could teach you a lot of things you've never heard of, doll.

Cheryl: Don't you be so rude. Come on Trace.

Spider: Hey listen, freak out, sugar. Come with us to Grantham.

Tracey *(coming up to the window of the cab):* Am I really being filmed?

Spider: Yeah, got it in one babe, you're going to be a star.

Vim: Come on, Spider.

Spider: Hold on. Look, come on. *(He opens the door.)* Listen, you'll be all right.

      Tracey starts to unload all her school stuff onto Cheryl.

Tracey: Tell me mum I'm round at your place.

Cheryl: Don't be so stupid, Trace, he's probably got a durex in his pocket.

Tracey: Well, I'll be all right then, won't I?

Cheryl: Trace!!

      Tracey gets into the van onto Spider's knee. The van lurches off.

Spider: Well this is a suprise, isn't it. Er, this is Colin this is Den, and this is Vim, What's your name?

Tracey: Trace.

Spider: Trace. Do you like Heavy Metal, Trace?

Tracey: Yeah, I love it.

● Numerous shots of the van heading towards the north and onto the A1, overlaid with another of the group's songs.

We pick up on a shot of an egg being cracked into a heavily oiled frying pan, and pull back across the kitchen of what is obviously a very greasy café.

Vim's Voice: Our lifestyles have got a lot better. I mean we're not rich yet, but it's obvious we're going to be. So, you know, we don't worry so much about money.

The camera moves through the kitchen door to behind the counter. Den is at the checkout.

Cashier: Two pounds and five pence please love.

Den: Two quid!

Cashier: That's right, two pounds and five pence please.

Den: Two quid for one bloody sausage!

Cashier: That's right, love. Two pounds and five pence. *(Den picks up the sausage in his hand.)*

Den: Right, where's the camera?

He looks round, finds the camera, then turns back to the cashier.

Look, what's the name of this place?

She doesn't answer. Den looks right into camera.

Well anyway, it's a rip off; they're charging two quid for one bloody sausage, so don't come here.

Cashier: It was clearly marked, love. 'Sausage beans and chips, two pounds and five pence'.

Den: I haven't got two quid. *(Pause)* Can I have half a sausage for a quid?

Cashier: No you can't.

● **Cut to shot of the band at one of the tables in the café. A very trendy journalist approaches and removes her sunglasses.**

Sally: Heh, Bad News!

Everybody turns to camera.

All: Hey! Sally Friedman!

As each of the following lines is spoken the speakers appear in single close-up shots.

Colin: Britain's number one sexy chick rock journalist.

Sally: What gives? Coast to coast tour?

Spider: Putting heavy metal back on the rock and roll map where it belongs.

Vim: A thousand and one smashed motel rooms.

Den: We're on . . . No I still can't read that thing from here.

● **Cut to shot of the group sitting round the table with Sally at the head.**

Den: Wait a minute, I was sitting over there.

Sandy's Voice: Carry on Den, carry on.

Den: No, no, it's not . . ., it's going to be wrong, you see. It's meant to join up with that last bit, isn't it?

Sandy's Voice: Yes.

Den: Yeah, that's what I thought. Well I was sitting over there then, right? Then how come I'm suddenly sitting over here? Now?

Vim: He's right, I was sitting over there.

● **There is a cut in the film but we come back to exactly the same shot, except that Vim and Den have changed places.**

Sally: O.K. Let's cut the 'your favourite films, books, records and funniest experiences' routine.

Den *(looking at the menu on the wall):* Wait a minute! It says 'sausages' up there, not just one sausage. *(He turns to the cashier who is clearing the next table.)* Look at that, look, it says 'sausages'. Where's me other sausage, then?

● **The band are in the carpark outside the cafeteria with Sally, they all amble slowly towards the camera.**

Sally: O.K. Let's cut the 'your favourite films books, records and funniest experience' routine and get down to the meat.

Den: Let me tell you my funniest experience first.

Vim: Shut up, Den.

Sally: First of all I've got to make my position clear, I'm in love with heavy metal. I know, I should have some ideological theory to renounce all the over-established musical forms as the worthless ego-massaging opiates they so obviously are. But that said, you've got to differentiate between the crass commercial glitter gonzos, and those who, though dismissed as unfashionable by casual chaps in this year's slacks, refuse to be bullied out of their belief in the fundamental values of popular music, and sweat at their own temperature. What side of the fence are you on?

There is a pause as Vim ponders his answer, then a truck parks in between the group and the camera.

● **Shot of the band, with Sally and Tracey, leaning against the large door of a garage.**

Vim: Right, er, about what you were saying before, it's a valid question don't get me wrong about that, but I think you're really starting out from the wrong point of view, because we're not basically a heavy metal band, we're a bit more subtle than that, aren't we Colin?

Colin: What?

Vim: We're a bit more subtle than that.

Colin: Yeah, we're subtle, but basically we're heavy metal, aren't we?

Spider: Colin's right, Vim, if we made a record it'd be so heavy you couldn't get it off the turntable.

Vim: Yeah, look, I know that. I know, but I mean, all I'm saying is we're just not just simple heavy metal, you know.

Den: I thought we were heavy metal.

Vim: Look I know we've got heavy roots, you know, and I mean . . . What I'm trying to say is that we're trying to progress a bit you know, we're trying to break a few barriers.

Den: Are we?

Vim: Yeah.

> *Pause.*

Sally: Carry on.

Vim: Um, well, I mean, if I relate it back to what you were saying; we're not sitting on a fence at all. We're trying to burn the fence down. And it's pretty stupid to sit on burning fence.

The small door within the large garage door that Vim is leaning on opens, and he falls through it out of sight.

● **Cut to shot of Vim, Sally and Colin sitting on the sofa in the back of the van. Den is driving, and Spider and Tracey are sitting next to him.**

Vim: There's no point in being shackled to some stupid label.

Spider: What if the label's EMI?

Colin: That's not the point, Vim. What she's saying is that the label's not important, it's just a convenient point of reference.

Vim: Here we go, Colin the college boy.

Colin: Well it's obvious. What's wrong with being heavy metal anyway? It was you that put 'heavy metal' in the advert, that's why I joined.

Den: Yeah, me too.

Vim: Yeah, I know I did, but things change, don't they? When I was a kid I used to play John Denver numbers all the time, but that doesn't mean I have to be a prat *all* my life.

Spider: You said it, Vim – hey listen, we could call ourselves 'Heavy Denver'.

Tracey: That's really funny Spider, 'Heavy Denver'.

Vim: Tell her to shut up or get out will you, Spider?

Spider: Shut up or get out.

　　　　Fade to black.

● **Caption; 'One and a half hours later'. Camera picks up on the same scene.**

Vim: Look, we're not just another stupid heavy metal band.

Colin: What about 'futuristic heavy metal'?

Vim: But we're more modern that futurisitic aren't we?

Spider: I know, what about 'Glitterbilly Heavy Romantic'?

　　　　Tracey laughs.

Tracey: Sorry, I forgot.

　　　　The van pulls into a layby.

Vim: What you doing, Den?

Den: Right, that's it, I'm getting out here if we're anything to do with the New Romantics.

　　　　Den gets out and slams the door.

● **Shot of Den standing on the roadside. The other band members approach him in a conciliatory fashion.**

Vim's Voice: One of the things about being the leader is that you've got to sort out arguments that come up between people in the group. You've got to be fair, and you've got to make sure your own ego doesn't get in the way.

Colin: Come on Den, it was only a joke.

Den: I don't care, I don't care if it was a joke or not.

Colin: Tell him.

Spider: It was a joke.

Den: I'm not going any further until I hear Alan say that we're heavy metal.

>   *Long pause.*

Spider: Come on, tell him, then.

Vim: O.K., O.K., we're Heavy Metal O.K.? Heavy Metal, Heavy Metal, Heavy Metal, have I said it enough? We're Heavy Metal, O.K.? Just like your fucking brain.

>   *As the rest of the band accept this statement and head back towards their van, Spider leers into the camera.*

Spider: This is heavy – geddit?

● **Shot of the van on the A1 from a bridge. As the van approaches it suddenly pulls off the road onto the verge.**

Sandy's Voice: What are they doing? Why can't they just do what they're bloody well told? Mark, give me the radio. Hello, why have you stopped?

>   *Den comes through on the radio.*

Den's Voice: Hello. We are receiving you loud and clear, over.

Sandy's Voice: Cut the jargon and just answer the question, you stupid bastard.

Vim's Voice: Look this is Vim here. Just watch who you're calling a stupid bastard O.K.? And for your information we've broken down, you stupid bastard.

>   *The camera has panned slowly from the van on the verge to Sandy standing on the bridge. Sandy clocks the camera.*

Sandy: Oliver, I am not the subject of this documentary, point the camera at the van.

● **Cut to a shot of Sandy, Den, Vim and people from the camera crew standing in between the broken down van, and the camera crew's plush Winnebago.**

Sandy: You can't use our bus.

Vim: But why not?

Sandy: Because it's your problem – you've got to handle it. We're just here to point the cameras O.K.? That's the whole point of documentaries. Look, don't worry, this is going to look really good in the film – it's great. It's really interesting, we're lucky it happened, actually.

Den: You're lucky I don't knock your fucking head in.

Sandy: There's no need to get violent is there? And try not to swear so much, please, for the sake of this film.

Den: You can always put in a fucking bleep can't you.

Sandy: Yes, yes, that's not the point though.

Vim: No, no, that's not the point is it? The point is how come you think you can interfere with the way we talk, and not interfere when the van's broken down?

Den: Yeah, right.

Vim: Answer that and stay fashionable.

Mark: Come on now let's keep cool.

Vim and Den: Fuck off!!

Mark: Don't talk to me like that..

Sandy: Cut it!

● **Shot of the Winnebago travelling along the A1. As it passes we realize that it is towing the band's van.**

Vim's Voice: It's obvious we're going to make it, I mean, we're the only band I know that can play a thirteen-bar boogie. I mean, all we've got to do is make a record and sell it, we'd be as rich as the Stones if we'd sold as many records as them.

> *Shot from inside the Winnebago. We see the van being towed along behind. The band notice that they are being filmed and drop their trousers.*

● **Shot outside the Roxy in Grantham. Sally is on the steps talking to the manager.**

Sally: Robbie, you've been manager of the Roxy for nearly fifteen years, this was the hunting…

> *Sally and the manager look round in alarm as they hear the sound of a horn. They jump out of the way just in time to avoid being mown down by the van.*

● **Shot of the manager's office. Den, Spider and Tracey are tucking into a little package of sandwiches and a bag of crisps.**

Den: Anyone want this last cheese one?

Tracey: There's not much is there?

Spider: No.

Tracey: And I thought they laid on like, you know, food and drink and that.

> *The manager pushes his way past the camera crew into the office.*

Manager: Excuse me. Um. What do you think you're doing?

Den: Heh?

Manager: This is my office. This is my office, you're not supposed to be in here.

Spider: Your office?

Manager: And what are you doing eating my tea?

Den: What?

Spider: Sorry mate, we thought this was the dressing room.

Manager: No, no, no. The dressing rooms are out there.

> *He points to the door. Spider looks out of the door.*

Spider: All I can see is the toilets.

Manager: Yes.

Spider: Oh, I see.

Den: Oh, not the bloody toilets again.

Manager: Look, I came to tell you they're ready for the sound check.

Den: Yeah, all right, look though, we've got to sort out this toilet business though, all right?

Manager: Right on, man.

> *Den and Spider leave. Tracey makes to leave. The manager blocks her path.*

Manager: You don't have to go yet, do you?

Tracey: What?

Manager: Listen love, sound checks are very boring.

> *The manager shuts the door in the camera's face.*

● **Cut to the band on stage, they are making a tremendous noise. Colin isn't playing. Vim has to shout to get the others to stop.**

Vim: Stop! Stop! Stop! You're supposed to come in there, Colin.

Colin: All I'm asking, Vim, is that you let me sing just one number.

Vim: I know, I know, and I say you can't.

Colin: Well it's just not fair.

Vim: Look, this is my band, so it's fair.

Colin: Well if that's how it is, it's my brother's P.A. and I say that you all can't use it.

Vim: Look the only reason you're in this band is because you've got the bloody P.A.

Colin: Well maybe I should take my P.A. to a band where I might be appreciated a little more.

Vim: Well it'd better be a band in Grantham then, cause it's not going back in my van.

Colin: Yes, which *I* paid for to have repaired!

> *The manager comes onto the stage.*

Manager: Oi, oi Lads! I'm afraid that's all there's time for.

> *He throws a large switch which cuts out the lights and the power supply.*
> *The camera creeps round a corner to find Colin on the phone.*

Colin: Mum? Mum? Yeah, could you take some library books back for me? Yeah, um, Blair's *Origins of Feudal Britain*, er, . . . *(Colin suddenly clocks the camera. Panic sweeps over his face.)* Quo, er, Motorhead, Saxon, er, Uriah Heep, sure, um, and loads of bands er, and you can quote me on that, sure, yeah, yeah O.K., thanks, er, goodbye, see you, huh, O.K., ciao, right, yeah. *(He puts down the receiver.)* Huh, another reporter.

● **Cut to shot of Spider playing a pintable. Sally is leaning over the machine talking to him.**

Sally: How did you get into the music business, Spider?

Spider: Well, I went down the Job Centre, and told them I wanted to blow their minds.

Sally: Do you always play the pintable before a gig?

Spider: No. You asked me to because you thought it'd make a nice shot.

> *He leers into the camera.*

● **Shot of Sally making her way into the gents lavatories, the camera follows her. She stops outside one of the cubicles.**

Sally: Den?

Den: Who's that?

Sally: It's Sally.

Den: What are you doing in here? This is the men's.

Sally: I've come to interview you.

Den: I'm on the toilet!

Sally: Why? Is that because you're nervous?

Den: Nervous? No. Oh, I see what you mean. You thought I was shitting bricks didn't you? Well I am but it's got nothing to do with nerves, it's just like this problem I've got. You'll know when I'm nervous 'cause I throw up.

● **Sally and Vim are sitting in a stairwell smoking a joint.**

Vim: Yeah, I know, because like I was born to be on stage you know.

> *He hands Sally the joint.*

Sally: Thanks. How do you know?

Vim: Well I mean, what do you do if you're multi-talented? I mean you can't just sit at home in a coma. I could have been a Michelangelo, I could have been a Wordsworth, Joe Bugner, anything.

Sally: Yeah.

Vim: Yeah.

Sally: This is strong stuff, isn't it?

Vim: Yeah, it certainly does the job all right, doesn't it?

> *Sally tries to hand the joint to one of the crew and slips down a step.*

Sally: I don't think I can stand up.

Vim: What?

Sally *(whispering in his ear):* Aren't you going to sleep with me tonight?

Vim: What?

> *Sandy moves into frame and takes the joint from Sally.*

Sandy: Sally, Sally. I thought you told me this thing was fake. *(He turns to camera and realises that it is still running.)* Oliver, what are you still running for?

Oliver's Voice: You haven't said 'Cut' yet.

Sandy: Well doesn't it appear a bit obvious sometimes?

Oliver's Voice: Well now, you said the art of making documentaries was to keep running all the time.

Sandy: Cut it. Please.

● **Den is throwing up in the corner of a corridor leading onto the stage. Sally and Spider look on.**

Sally: You nervous now, Den?

Den: No, I think it must be something I ate.

Spider: Urgh. Looks like everything you ate.

> *Vim comes round the corner.*

Vim: Come on we've got to get on stage now. God, Den, what's happening? Come on man.

> *Vim walks past the camera.*

Spider *(into camera):* Rock 'n' Roll man.

> *Spider walks past the camera.*

Den *(into the camera):* Sorry.

> *Den walks past the camera.*

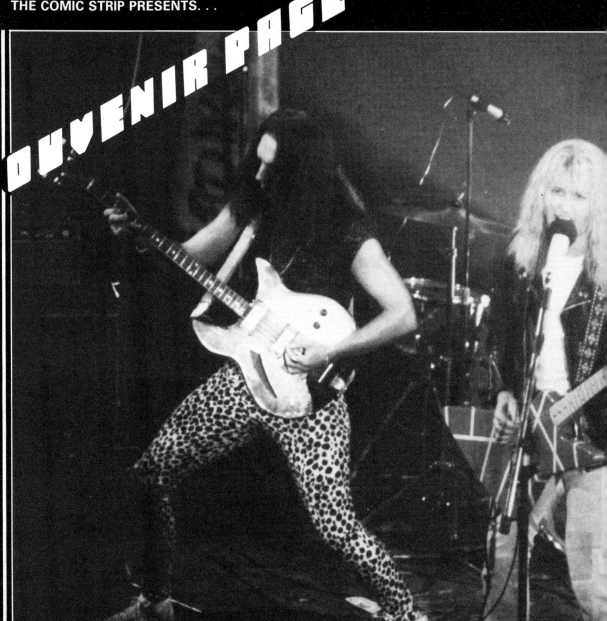

SOUVENIR PAGE

● **The band are on stage.**

Vim: One, two, three, four.

> *The band launch into their first number. The gig is covered by two cameramen who move around the stage at an alarming speed, getting ridiculously unimaginative 'Top of the Pops' angles on everything in sight. Vim sings.*

Look out, I'm out of control,
Look out, I'm out of control,
Look out, I'm out of control,
I said, Look out I am Rock 'n' roll.

> *The volume of the concert is turned down and we hear Vim's voice from a previously recorded interview laid over the top.*

Vim's Voice: I think I can handle fame, I mean, I think I'm ready for it, you know. I mean, I've had fame before, because I was on 'Opportunity Knocks' when I was a kid. It was when I was eleven. I did 'Purple Haze' on the acousitc guitar, er, with my dad on the trumpet. It was a bit naff I suppose, but I mean, it was good experience.

The volume of the concert is turned up and we hear the words of one of the verses.

I am the rock, I am the rock,
I am like an electric shock,
I am the roll, I am the roll,
Watch me, I drink alcohol.

The volume cuts out again as Vim's voice comes to the fore.

Vim's Voice: We've got quite a following now, you know. Not me and my dad, I mean the band, you know. You can't beat a good live band, I mean, I just live for playing live. I'd do it for free if I didn't need the money.

The sound of the concert predominates momentarily so that we can hear Vim's excruciating lead break. Then we return to Vim's voice.

The buzz, the buzz that you get off the audience is amazing. I mean, it's the audience that makes a gig, you know. When you're on stage there, and there's this huge crowd of people, all sweating and jumping about, and all enjoying themselves, and it's all because of you.

The song comes to a climactic end with a series of crescending chords. The camera pulls round onto the audience which comprises Tracey, three others and a small dog. Tracey goes apeshit with adulation. The dog yawns.

Vim: We'd like to do our next number now called 'Businessman'. One, two, three, four.

> *The picture fades to black and the music fades.*

● **The band are on stage after the gig, they are clearing up the equipment. The manager comes to the edge of the stage.**

Manager: Heh Lads! Heh Lads! I just wanted to say it was a great gig. Tremendous.

Colin: Well, thanks very much. Did you think that when I came. . .

Vim: What about the money?

> *The manager doesn't answer.*

What about the money?

Manager: Sorry, I'm afraid there isn't any.

Vim: What?

Manager: Well you saw them out there tonight didn't you? Four people.

Spider: Hey – don't forget the dog.

Den: Yeah. You didn't let the dog in free did you?

Vim: I don't understand. We were on a straight forty quid, there was no box office or nothing.

Manager: Look, I said I'm sorry didn't I? I'll go and check it out O.K.?

> *The manager runs off.*

● **Cut to a shot of the band on stage having obviously packed up all their gear. Colin enters frame.**

Vim: Well?

Colin: Can't find him. He must have buggered off.

Vim: Bastard.

Tracey: It's not his fault, I think he's quite nice.

Colin: You shut up you tart. He's trying to get out of paying me.

Tracey: Well that bloke told him not to.

Vim: What?

Tracey: He told him not to pay you.

Den *(indicating Sandy)*: What him?

Vim: What? Is that right?

> *Sandy moves into frame.*

Sandy: Look, don't worry, you'll get your money. I was just trying to make it a bit more interesting, you know, create a bit of conflict.

> *Vim jumps off the stage to confront Sandy.*

Vim: Yeah. Well, if it's conflict you're looking for. . .

> *He punches Sandy.*

Sandy: Look don't do that.

Vim: And who's going to stop me, heh?

> *He hits him again.*

Sandy: Get the police, Mark!

Vim: Get the camera, Den!

> *A large-scale fight ensues. Vim punching Sandy who is on the floor. Den pulling the camera away from the camera man, and Spider and Colin relieving the soundman of his equipment.*

Sandy: Keep rolling, Oliver! Keep rolling!

Colin: We've got the sound gear. Look, let's get up to the office and lock ourselves in – make up our own documentary.

> *The camera spins round and goes dead.*

● **The screen is blank. We hear the band in the manager's office.**

Spider's Voice: O.K. I think the taperecorder's working, it's going round anyway.

Vim's Voice: Come on, Colin.

Den's Voice: Why don't you let me help you?

Colin's Voice: Look just keep your hands off it, Den.

Den's Voice: What about that button there?

> *The camera comes on. Blurred close-up of Den's face.*

Den: Yeah, there you are, look. I can hear it now, it must be on.

Colin's Voice: All right, all right, so it's on. Can you just get back? I'm trying to get it in focus.

> *Den moves back. Vim joins him.*

Vim: Come on, Spider.

> *Spider moves into frame with the tape recorder slung around his neck, headphones on, holding the microphone, Den shouts into the microphone.*

Den: Hello, Spider!

Spider: Brilliant joke, Den.

Den: Thanks.

> *Colin moves into the picture.*

Vim: Right. Now does everyone know what they're doing?

Den: Yeah, I just say, 'Heavy metal, top of the class, stuff the media up your arse'.

Spider: Yeah, and don't forget to get your cock out, Den.

Den: Heh?

Vim: Look, don't confuse him Spider.

> *The camera falls over on its side.*

Colin: Hang on, it's fallen over.

Vim: Come on! Get it together for Christ's sake!

Colin: Look will you stop shouting at me, Alan, it's beginning to get on my tits.

Vim: Piss off. And stop calling me 'Alan'.

Colin: All right then, Ajax, or whatever you new name is.

> *The film goes dead. The sound continues.*

Vim's Voice: Don't you dare wind me up.

Den's Voice: I think it's run out of film.

Colin's Voice: What?

Den's Voice: Yeah, we've run out of film.

Colin's Voice: Oh God.

Den's Voice: It's all right, there's some more over here in this can.

> *We hear the sound of a film can being opened.*

Colin's Voice: Den! Don't touch . . . What did you go and do that for?

Den's Voice: What?

Colin's Voice: Never take new film out of a tin. We've got no film left now, it's a complete waste of time.

Den's Voice: Oh, I'll put it back then.

Vim's Voice: God Den, you're stupid. *(Pause)* You know what?

Colin's Voice: What?

Vim's Voice: This band is a pile of shit.

Den's Voice: Heh?

Spider's Voice: Hang on everybody, we're going to run out of tape soon. Yeah, here it comes, any moment . . . . . now!

> *Long pause.*

No, hang on, I was wrong, it's going to be about . . .

Written by Adrian Edmondson

CAST					
Vim	Adrian Edmondson	**Sally**	Jennifer Saunders	**Sandy**	Sandy Johnson
Den	Nigel Planer	**Cheryl**	Serena Evans	**Oliver**	Oliver Stapleton
Colin	Rik Mayall	**Neighbour**	Bert Parnaby	**Mark**	Mark Cooper
Spider	Peter Richardson	**Manager**	Neville Smith		
Tracey	Dawn French	**Girlfriend**	Judy Hawkins		
		Cashier	Chara Bala Choski	Directed by Sandy Johnson	

Summer

School

Liz is driving Peter in a 2CV, a happy couple. The car proceeds up a drive and approaches a university building. They park and get out.

Liz and Peter enter the foyer. There are already long lines of people waiting to register for their particular courses (eg. Acupuncture, Lancashire Mythology, Furniture History etc.). The co-ordinator, Julian, is wandering around, greeting everyone. Beth and Jake are in the Iron- Age Village queue. Jake looks very ill.

Beth I wish you would stop whining, the fresh air will do you a world of good.

Jake Beth, I am a seriously ill person, please try and understand . . .

> *They reach the desk.*

Julian Ah, right. *(He ticks them off on his list.)* If you could just fill in these forms and bring them back here when you've finished? Then we can register you officially.

Beth Thank you.

> *They move away.*

Tark Hi! Julian

Julian Oh God.

Tark Can't keep me away, can you!

Julian Hello, Tarquin.

Tark The usual, is it? . . . *(He picks up a form.)* Nick around?

> *Julian points to Nick, who is chatting up one of the girls.*

Nick Susan, God you know something? That was my mother's name . . .

Tark Nick!

Nick Tark! Excuse me, Sarah, – how are you, you son of a gun?

Tark Pretty good, you know, keeping fit *(makes a 'fuck' gesture)* . . . seen any of the, er, "women" this year?

Nick Not yet, not yet – slowly, slowly catchee pussy.

Tark Or 'catchee crabs'! Remember Nancy?

Nick Keep your voice down.

> *Ursula passes to join the queue. Outside a Morgan car pulls up. Simon and Desmond get out. Desmond wears a large greatcoat and spats.*

Nick Ah, Ursula, great to have you along again – hope you *enjoy* this year as much as last year, eh?!! *(Winks.)*

Ursula Piss off, bollock features. Hello Tark.

> *She joins the queue.*

Tark Hi!

>   *Tark drops his bag and loads of tools fall out.*

Peter Peter Fielding . . .

Liz . . . and Liz Gedding.

Julian If you could just fill out these forms . . .

Peter Rightio, thanks.

Ursula Hello Julian – how are you?

Julian Urs! God, you've changed . . .

Ursula Yes, I'm a natural blonde these days.

Julian *(hands her a form)* You know the routine.

Ursula Thanks.

>   *Beth and Jake are talking.*

Jake Why don't I go home – I'll pick you up at the end of next week . . .?

>   *In the queue.*

Simon Oh yeah, right, great, fine, super.

Julian Great.

Desmond I wish to join the others in the quest for survival . . .

Julian Sorry?

Desmond I want to return to the soil . . .

Julian If you could fill out one of these.

>   *Standing behind Desmond are the perfect, beautiful couple, in Fiorrucci clothes, arm in arm.*
>   *Tarzan and Jane.*
>
>   *Ursula strides up to the desk, and gives back the form.*

Ursula Here you are, Julian – is it the same changing room?

Julian Yes, here's your key.

The locker room.
Ursula enters. Tark, Liz and Peter, Beth and Jake are already there. Tark is already changed.

Tark *(to Peter)* There's your locker there.

Peter Oh yes, thanks.

Tark Don't forget to put it all on – there's no "oh dear, I forgot my leggings" later y'know. You can't come back.

Peter Ah, yes.

Tark Thank God these are a bit tighter than the ones I had last year – my balls kept falling out for everyone to see – looked like a Neanderthal petrol pump. Ha! Bloody cold though, I can tell you!

Liz I wonder if it would be all right if I kept my bra on? I don't usually take it off . . .

Tark Don't be so pathetic, woman, get it off, there's nothing to be embarrassed about, we're all going to *see a lot of each other* in the next few weeks, if you get my meaning. Ha!

Liz Well, I know, but . . .

Tark Tell me, did Iron-Age woman have Playtex to guide her? Not on your life – get it off, for Christ's sake. I give up with all you fallen feminists.

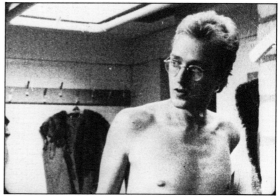

Beth *(to Liz)* It's leg stubble that will bother me . . . and what about . . . *(whispers)* Tee Ay Em Pee Ay Ex.

> *Julian enters.*

Julian Everything OK in here? Got everything you need? Of course, there are some tools down in the village from last year but I hope you all understand that you are totally self-sufficient otherwise, so you won't be needing *this*, Tark.

> *He takes a Black and Decker chainsaw from him.*

Tark *(whispers)* Shit.

> *He goes out. Desmond enters, meaningful looks.*
>
> *Ursula approaches Peter. Beth and Liz are talking. Jake is very pissed off, none of his clothes fit.*

Ursula *(very close to Peter's face)* So, Pete . . .

Peter Peter, I prefer Peter.

Ursula Yes, I think I might prefer Peter too, to all the other men here . . .

Peter Oh, really? Well, that's nice. And . . . er . . . what's your name?

Ursula Ursula, but you can call me Ursula. No, seriously, call me Urs.

Peter Urs. Right.

Ursula Tell me Peter . . .

Peter Yes?

Ursula Is your seed plenteous?

Tark Well, I'm ready. I'm going to sink my last pint for a fortnight – anyone care to join me for a tipple? *(They studiously ignore him.)*

> Righto – see you later. *(He goes out.)*

In the student's bar. Lots of students. Ursula is on the Space Invaders.

Nick *(dressed in skins, to the barman)* Excuse me, Paul, could I have a cinzano and lemonade for Wendy?

Japanese Girl Wey, Wey actually.

Nick Of course, Wey, Wey, what a lovely name . . . for a lovely lady.

Tark *(pushing in – shouts)* Pint of real ale!

Simon Hang on a sec.

> *Tarzan and Jane with big cocktails with umbrellas, cherries etc. Beth and Jake are still complaining.*
>
> *Liz and Peter enter, feeling very silly and shy. They hold hands and walk to the bar, where Desmond is sitting.*

Liz Hello, you must be one of us.

Peter *(laughing at Liz's joke)* Ha,ha! Yes, yes.

Desmond If by that you mean we are to be fellow travellers on the path of knowledge about our forefathers then, yes, I am 'one of you'.

Liz Ah good. I'm Liz and this is Peter.

Desmond I am Lug, son of Mil.

Peter *(awkward)* Ah.

On a grassy bank outside a bunch of "villagers" stumble by, well-oiled, looking for the huts. In the foreground, hidden, we see Nick and the Japanese girl groping.

Gradually, all the villagers assemble in the main hut – a motley crew of different shapes and sizes. There is an oil lamp on the floor.

Tark grunts and collapses on the floor in an inebriated heap. Everyone is a bit embarrassed.

Julian enters.

Julian Ah good, everyone here then? *(He does a loud head count. Gets it wrong)* Sorry could you stand still for *just* a sec? Thanks. *(Another head count)* Right, great, everyone's here!

> *Nick enters, bedraggled.*

Nick Sorry, am I late?

Julian Ah, *now* everyone's here. Well, I'll leave you to it. Don't forget that there is a small crops garden we've planted just to get you started. 'Fraid I can't tell you where it is, though, you'll have to find it.

He picks up the lamp.

Have to take this as well, I'm afraid. No mod cons and all that. I'll pop in from time to time to keep a check on things. Good luck everyone and happy hunting!

He goes out. The hut is plunged into darkness.

Liz   I s'pose we'd better try and get a fire going – has anyone got any flints?

Simon   I've got my lighter.

Everyone tuts.

Sorry.

Tark farts.

Morning. Panavision sunrises. For the first time we see the village properly. It is in the middle of some modern concrete buildings. Ordinary university students wander across the quad, through the village, to their various classes.

Villagers are asleep in the hut. Tark is woken by the students' chatter. He rushes out of the main hut.

Tark   Shut up you bastards! Can't you see we're trying to sleep for Christ's sake?!

He goes back inside.

Liz   Tark! Come back in!

Tark   I think they got the message.

Liz   Calm down, Tark. Come and sit down. We must work out some kind of plan for the day and certain policies for the village in general.

Simon   Yeah, right.

Beth   Very good idea.

Peter   Absolutely. Moral codes are very important.

Tarzan and Jane appear at the door.

Liz   Morning!

They smile and join the circle of villagers.

I mean, are we going to allow people to walk through the village at random?

Simon   P'raps we should ask Julian to keep them away?

Nick sits very close to Ursula.

Nick   *(whispering)* Come on Urs. Let bygones be bygones, last year was a big mistake for both of us. Friends?!

Ursula   Get away from me, you syphillitic scab.

Tark I think we should kill anyone we catch.

Peter Steady on, Tark.

Tark This is our territory and we must protect it. Scalping is the most effective method, apparently.

Liz I don't think we should call Julian in on this unless it's absolutely necessary.

Ursula Right.

Simon Oh, yeah.

Tark We should go ahead and *attack* if we feel threatened.

Beth But Tark, no-one is threatening us.

Tark Aha, exactly! Very clever tactics yes – it's quite clear to me that we should attack *before* being threatened in this case.

Jake Beth! *(Loud whisper)* Beth! – feel my forehead, it's burning!

Beth *(embarrassed)* Shhhh!

Liz Can I make a suggestion?

Ursula Please do, so long as it's sensible.

Peter Go on.

Liz Thank you. Well, I think we can use body language.

Nick Yes, make our bodies speak.

   He looks at Ursula.

Beth How do you mean?

Liz Well, by the way we stand, sit and move around – aggressively for instance, they will understand that this is our space.

Simon Right.

Ursula Great idea, now can we think about important things like food?

Beth Yes, I was just going to say –

Peter How about Simon and I going to search for this crops garden that Julian was talking about?

Liz Great.

Beth I can look for berries.

Liz I'll make a fire to cook on.

Tark I'll go and hunt for wild boar . . .

Jake I've got a bit of gyppy tummy actually, I think I'd better lie down for a while.

   They go outside. Nick goes over to Liz.

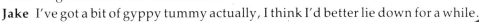

Nick How about if I help you get *some heat* going, Jean?

Liz Liz.

Nick Sorry, Liz. Strange that I should call you Jean – that was my mother's name and she died in a car crash last year.

Liz Oh, I'm sorry.

Nick Just for a moment there, your wild earthiness reminded me of her. Now what about this fire? We'll need some friction . . .

> *Ursula butts in.*

Ursula Oh Nick, how kind of you to offer to go and fetch *the wood*, whilst Liz and I prepare the fire. *THANK YOU!!*

> *Nick slinks off.*

And you Desmond? Sorry, "Lug son of Mil" . . . what are you going to do?

Desmond I am going in search of the sacred mushroom.

> *He goes out.*

Scenes of activity on the campus.

Tark with spear is hunting for boar in a corridor. Simon and Peter find the crops garden – it is pathetic, three floppy cabbages and various vegetables in a row. About six foot square. Tarzan and Jane are walking in the trees, looking glamorous.

Jake is lying down in the main hut. Ursula and Liz are trying to build a fire.

Ursula You see, the problem is that men are weak, weak in flesh and weak in spirit. That's why I couldn't bear the thought of marriage, but I do want to have children – that's why I must find a suitable mate, just for reproduction.

Liz I think you're a very strong person Ursula, I really do.

> *Ursula gives up with the fire and goes to sit at the loom, a complete mess of tangles.*

Ursula Don't get me wrong. I do *like* men, but only now and then y'know. Mind you, I am feeling ripe for a child at the moment . . .

> *Tark enters with a dead crow.*

Night. Everyone is sitting around in the main hut, eagerly awaiting the outcome of the bubbling pot in the middle. Liz serves up the disgusting green food. Silence. People try to eat it. Jake rushes out and throws up. Tarzan and Jane get up and walk out, smiling. Beth is spoonfeeding Jake.

Morning. Long shot of the campus.
A lone student wanders across the village. Suddenly Tark rushes out, clubs him and drags
him off to one of the smaller huts. Simon is working on a roof.
Desmond is building a phallic symbol – he walks to the main hut.
Ursula is in a tub, Beth is pouring on hot water from the fire. Liz is cutting cabbages. Peter is
trying to mould a pot from clay. Desmond is very close to him. Jake is curled up in pain on
the floor.

Liz It's just that I feel very strongly that we have come here with more knowledge of language
and communication than we should have . . .

Ursula But we can't do anything about that now.

Beth We can't pretend we don't know how to speak . . .

Jake is writhing around on the floor.

Ursula More water Beth – I must prepare my body for the sacred conception.

Liz Exactly, we can't pretend that we have no language, so we must invent our own, you
know, with grunts and things.

Ursula Eensy bit *Quest for Fire* – Desmond Morris, don't you think love?

Liz I'll show you . . .

She grunts a whole sentence.
Simon falls through the roof.

Liz See!

Simon Well, no, actually.

She tries again.

Simon Ah.

Liz What do you think it was?

Simon Something about Germany?

Liz No, no, no.

She tries again.

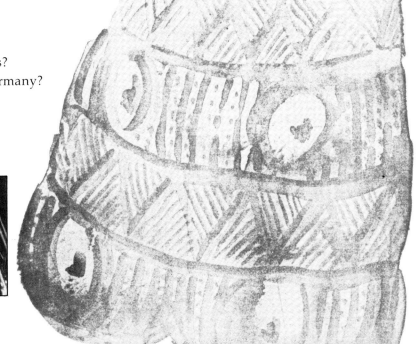

Ursula is making eyes at Peter, who is very embarrassed. Desmond notices.

Desmond Like Queen Maeb, she radiates light and warmth, but when the traveller comes close to enjoy the heat, he falls prey to her spider's web and, even though the warmth feels good, it is the warmth of the fires of hell!!! Lug too, had a wife who proved unfaithful to him with Kermat, son of Dagda. Lug killed Kermat with his magic staff.

Peter Really?

Desmond There is a lesson here for all of us to learn, is there not?

Peter Yes, oh yes, I'm sure there is.

By the stream. Tark and Tarzan are fishing. Tark comes up with a durex on the end of his stick. Behind them, Jane is standing against a tree seductively and Nick is trying to chat her up.

Nick Jane? God, that's strange, I had an identical twin sister called Jane . . . She was killed when our pram crashed, I tried to save her but . . .

Tarzan strides up with a trout in his hands. Nick slinks off.

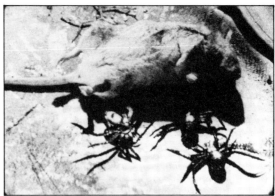

In the hut. One by one, the villagers bring the day's offerings for lunch. It is mostly grass and roots. Tark puts a pile of slugs down. It is pathetic and they are all depressed. They are all trying the grunting language.

Tark Oh Christ! Shut up! That's it – I haven't eaten a decent meal with *meat* for three days, I'm going up to the canteen.

Simon Oh come on Tark, that's not exactly cricket!

Beth Yes, don't give up.

Tark But I'm ravenous and all we've got is bloody grass.

Liz We can make a *lovely* stew from this.

     Jake throws up.

Simon What about all those rabbits you said were around, Tark?

Tark I . . . they . . . well . . . myxamatosis, I s'pose.

Ursula I know where there are loads of rabbits . . .

A huge laboratory full of experimental white rabbits in cages. The villagers coming out, students walk by. They whistle innocently – rabbits under each arm.

In the main hut at night.
Jake is very ill and sweating.
They have all finished the rabbits and are full and happy. A lot of home-made booze going round. Some are grunting.

Simon Well done girls, jolly good meal.

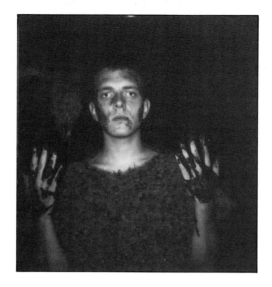

Tark *I* killed them!
> *He is covered in blood and fur.*

Beth Yes, well done, Tark. I think . . .?
> *She applauds him and the others join in.*

Liz Shall we *all* have a try at the new language?

Tark Stupid idea, we've got much more important things to think about.

Peter Like what?

Tark Like where we're all sleeping tonight.

Ursula Yes!

Liz Sorry?

Tark I mean sex.

Simon What?!

Ursula Yes!

Tark Well, we all have needs and I happen to have more than most . . .
> *Pause.*

We are supposed to be living as close to the idea of Iron Age culture as possible, aren't we?

Liz Well, yes.

Tark And they must have 'slept around' quite a bit in those days, otherwise there wouldn't have been any more little Iron-Age people, would there?

Ursula No.
> *Silence.*

Tark So we ought to follow suit.

Ursula Yes.
> *Silence.*

Liz I hate to say it, but of course he's right. We can't do this thing by half measures.

Nick Yes, we must do this properly.

Tark I think it's best if we shag all the girls in turn, that's the most democratic thing . . . So who is with me tonight, then?
> *Silence.*

Gradually, although embarrassed, people start to pair off. Tarzan and Jane walk out together, very fast.

Simon *(very quiet)* Er, Liz, perhaps we could . . . ?

Liz Yes, of course, Simon, I'd love to.

She glances at Peter who is completely overwhelmed and Simon and Liz go out.

Ursula strides up to Peter and takes his hand.

Ursula Come on, Peter. You are my chosen one.

Peter But . . .

Ursula No buts about it. We'll go to one of the smaller huts, so's we can be alone.

They go out.

Nick Well, Linda . . .

Beth Beth.

Nick Beth, of course. How strange . . . Beth, I want you to know that what you and I are about to do is all in the course of duty. We *must* take on the responsibility of research.

Beth Yes, I suppose you're right . . . Only one snag.

Nick What's that?

Beth I'm having my Pee Ee Ar Eye Owe Dee, I think we should wait a few days – bit mucky, y'know.

Nick *(confused)* "Pernod?!"

Tark is left alone, all save for Jake who is throwing up violently in the corner.

Desmond slowly gets up and walks out.

A caravan is parked discreetly on the campus.
Tarzan and Jane are in it getting undressed. She has face cream and carmen rollers. He has a smoking jacket on and a glass of port in his hand.
Ursula and Peter are in the small hut.

Ursula I'm so glad we've got the opportunity to do this, Peter, you were the one that I chose right from the start.

Peter You mean you knew this would happen?

Ursula Oh yes, we do it every year, but I have a special quest.

Peter Sorry?

Ursula This year I am going to conceive a strong warrior man-child, Peter, and that child will be yours.

Peter Well, I'm not exactly sure . . .

Ursula Your manhood will explode within me and my maidenhood will join with it in perfect union and we will create a new, magnificent being and he shall be called ''Son of Peter''.

> *Desmond enters.*

Desmond Daughter of Maeb!! I chastise you for your faithlessness. You are wife of Bran, second son of Odin and you bring plague and disease.

Ursula What?!

Desmond Get gone from here! Else I shall use my magic staff to remove you.

Ursula Shut up, Desmond, and piss off . . . Now, Peter.

> *Desmond raises a huge phallic club.*

Ursula All right, all right, I'm going!

> *She gets up.*

One of these years, Desmond, . . . I'm going to have your goolies for marbles.

Desmond Begone! Foul temptress!

> *She runs out.*

Ursula Bastard! Bloody pervert! I'm going to find some REAL men.

> *She stomps off towards the university.*

Desmond Peter, you must be puzzled.

Peter Well, I . . .

Desmond Relax, my friend and remember the fate of the traveller – the fires of hell?

Peter Oh yes . . . well . . . thank you very much for saving me.

Desmond Lie down, Peter, and relax, for you must retain your strength – sleep, sleep, draw those heavy curtains across your eyes.

> *Peter lies down and closes his eyes.*
> *Rear view of Desmond.*

Desmond Peter.

Peter Yes.

Desmond Would you like to see how the magic staff works?

Peter *(sleepily)* Yes, that would be very nice.

> *Desmond drops his trousers . . .*

Morning. Beth and Nick are asleep, a good few yards between them.

Nick *(in his sleep)* . . . and lots of doo doos, Mummy.

> *In the main hut Tark is fast asleep and snoring. Nearby, Jake is lying with his bottom up in the air and his trousers half off.*
> *Peter and Liz are sitting together on the quad, near the phallic symbol Desmond has been building. They whisper.*

Peter So you don't mind then?

Liz Well, when Tark first suggested it, I was a bit shocked, I must say . . . but . . .

Peter But?

Liz But I now realize how important it is to do this thing properly and if it means sharing each other . . . sexually, even if I don't like it . . . that is what we must do.

Peter Did you . . . enjoy it?

Liz Peter!

Peter No, I want to know, did you?

Liz Well . . .

Peter I mean, was he better than . . . well . . . you know . . . me?

Liz It's so difficult to compare.

Peter What do you mean?!

Liz He's a completely different sort of person to you and . . .

Peter What?!

Liz And I don't love *him*.

Peter *(relieved)* Oh Liz . . . I missed you so much last night.

Liz Oh, I would have thought you would have a great time with Ursula . . . I really like her.

Peter Yes, *she's* great . . . but . . .

Liz Oh come on, grumpy drawers, I'm going to try out the new language on everybody.

> *She starts to grunt at him.*

> Gosh, you know I really am enjoying this course . . . I don't know if it's the fresh air or what, but I feel quite gay . . . *(Peter looks shocked.)*

> *She starts to dash around like Isadora Duncan.*

Liz and Peter enter the main hut. The others gradually come in. Ursula enters, smiling like a Cheshire cat.

Liz *(grunt grunt.)*

Tark What?

Liz *(grunt grunt.)*

Tark Don't know what the fuck you're trying to say.

Liz I said 'Good Morning Tarquin'.

> *She grunts again to demonstrate.*

Tark *(grunt, grunt.)*

Liz I didn't quite get *that* one . . .

Tark I said 'Piss off'.

Liz Well that's charming, what's wrong with you this morning?

Tark *(sulks)* Nothing.

Liz Come on what is it, Tark?

Tark Well, I had to spend the whole night in here on my own, while you all went off to bonk.

Liz Jake was here, wasn't he?

Tark Yes, but . . .

    Scream from Beth.

Beth Oh my God!

Simon What is it?

Beth Jake, he doesn't seem to be . . . moving.

Peter What?!

Beth I think he's . . .

    Simon goes over.

Simon He's rather dead, I'm afraid.

    Silence.

    Beth starts to wail.

Peter He *did* say he wasn't feeling well.

Liz What a strange position . . .

Tark Oh Christ . . . I didn't think . . .

Simon *(realization)* Tark!

Peter Oh golly, Julian is heading this way.

Ursula Quick, hide Jake.

Liz What?!

Simon Where?

Peter Prop him up, sit him in the circle.

Ursula Hurry!

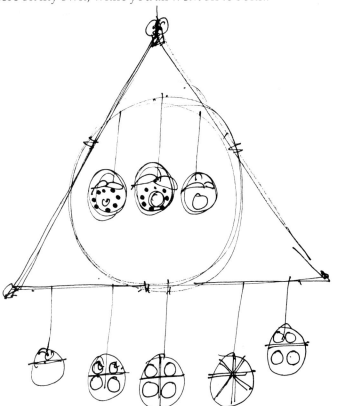

    They prop up the stiff and sit in a very close circle. Beth is distraught. Julian enters.

Julian Hi Gang!

    Silence.

What's this? Meditation time? Meditate with mother?

    Liz starts to grunt, the others pick up the idea pretty quickly and follow suit.

If you'd like to listen for just a sec . . . it's about the party.

    They continue to grunt.

Sorry, everyone, please, some hush?

    They grunt. Beth is wailing.

I see, that's the way we're playing the game, is it? I am trying to be reasonable . . .

    They grunt. Beth sobs.

You're just making it worse for everyone . . . somebody had better talk properly soon . . .

Beth Julian!! It's Jake . . . he's

    Tark gets up and coshes her out of sight of Julian. She falls back into Ursula's arms. She is out cold.

    They all smile

Julian Right, that's it . . . I've had enough of your silly game. What is the point? Try to help people
– won't even help themselves. O.K, O.K. It's not very clever actually. You'll see.

He goes out. They all laugh. He pops his head back in.

And if you think you're invited to the leaving do and disco – well – you're not.

He leaves. They all do "Ooo, nasty" noises.

Simon What are we going to do?

Liz I really don't know.

Peter I s'pose we ought to notify someone.

Ursula She'll have a headache when she comes round.

Tark Sorry, I just thought she might . . .

Desmond's voice booms out.

Desmond I, son of Mil, move that we build a funeral pyre, noble and high, that he may be burned and returned to the soil from whence he came.

Ursula A human sacrifice!

Simon Well, I don't know.

Liz It's what we *should* do, I suppose.

Peter Why don't we just call the ambulance?

Ursula I could make fertility symbols from his teeth.

Liz I suppose the ashes *would* make great clay . . .

Simon And we could dance around the fire.

Liz Desmond, sorry, Lug – would you lead the ritual for us?

Desmond Of course – but Peter, the innocent, must be my assistant.

They all look at him.

Evening. The villagers are all helping to build the pyre, Desmond supervises. Even Beth helps, although she is totally shocked and almost catatonic.

People in the university stare out of the windows at them, very puzzled.

Night. The villagers are sat in a large circle in the main hut, with the dead body in state in the centre. They are all humming.

At a mock altar, Desmond and Peter are concocting a potion with the mushrooms. They are facing away and they are naked.

When they turn round, we see that they have painted their willies and chests. Desmond struts around whilst Peter is incredibly embarrassed, Desmond mutters Gaelic mumbo-jumbo and administers the potion to everyone in turn. They get up and move around ritualistically – keep bumping into each other.

Gradually, everyone gets very high and they start to hum loudly. Desmond shouts:

Desmond Fire! Children of Odin!

And they all rush out, madly. Simon and Tarzan drag the body out.

Complete hysteria.
The body is dragged on to the top of the pyre and the whole thing is set alight and goes up in huge flames. The villagers are completely carried away and they dance around, shouting and screaming.
Students in the university look on in horror. Fire engines arrive and start to put out the flames. silhouetted on the top of one of the university buildings we see Nick and Ursula bonking away furiously. One of the firemen aims his hose at them. Ursula loves this and they bonk even harder.

Ursula Give me a child!!

Nick I'm coming mummy, I'm coming!!

The final day. They are all saying goodbye.
Peter and Desmond are whispering fond nothings. So are Liz and Simon. When they have finished this, they wave goodbye to each other and we see Simon and Desmond go arm in arm towards their car.
Liz and Peter get into their 2CV. Nick and Ursula come over as the happy couple and kiss them goodbye.
Jane and Tarzan wave goodbye from their Mercedes with the caravan behind.
We drive away inside Peter and Liz's car as we approached. They are very happy.
Then we see that the whole village is reduced to ash. Julian is walking around, knee-deep in it all, crying.
Beth is collecting bones.

Beth   Jake? Where are you Jake?
        Julian approaches, angry.
Julian   What the bloody hell has happened here. Where's Tark?. . . I bet he's got something to do with this . . . We've been running this course successfully for five years. . . .
        He throws his paper into the air.
        Well, I suppose that's it then.

We see the sun setting over the university building.

Written by Dawn French

CAST		Jake	Gerard Ryder	Desmond	Robbie Coltrane
Liz	Jennifer Saunders	**Tark**	Rik Mayall	**Japanese Girl**	Megumi
Peter	Adrian Edmondson	**Nick**	Peter Richardson	**Tarzan**	Martin Potter
Julian	Nigel Planer	**Ursula**	Dawn French	**Jane**	Elaine Ashley
Beth	Lois Baxter	**Simon**	R Frazer	Directed by Sandy Johnson	

"BACK TO NORMAL WITH EDDIE MONSOON"

A STUDIO LOUNGE SET with leather armchairs, tatty sofa,
a coffee table littered with empty bottles and full
ashtrays. A cocktail bar is on the right, complete
with microwave oven. On the back wall there is a door
leading to a hallway. On the left there is a drinks
cabinet and a picture display. The lounge is full of
gaudy colours (wallpaper) and plastic palms.

EDDIE MONSOON, completely pissed, is strapped in a
wheelchair in the centre of the room.

EDDIE: Good evening you bastards. I'm
            Eddie Monsoon and this is my
            television show.

                Holds up a whisky bottle.

            This is my bottle of whisky. These
            are my cigarettes and these are my
            so-called friends.

                CUT TO:

DOUG and LIONEL PRESCOTT by the drinks cabinet.
EDDIE continues in the background --

                'my matches, my'... etc.

LIONEL: Evening, viewers. How you doing?

                Raises a glass of sherry.

            I'm Lionel Prescott and this is my
            brother Douglas Prescott.

DOUG: Hello.

LIONEL: Sherry, Doug?

DOUG: Don't mind if I do, Lionel.

                BACK TO EDDIE.

EDDIE: My hobbies are: drinking, smoking, swearing,
            and grouse shooting. I am not a cripple
            and I don't believe in self control. I
            hate: soft drinks, racing drivers, so-called
            lasting friendships, everyone who lives
            on the Isle of Wight, last orders, blind
            people and stupid hard faced cows who say
            they'll do it and then don't, even when
            they're pissed.

                CUT TO:

VAG and CLITTY, standing by the cocktail bar. VAG
knocks over a sherry bottle.

VAG: Hello I'm Vag.

CLITTY: And I'm Clitty.

EDDIE: (VO)   Slags.

CLITTY: I want to talk to you... about alcoholism.

EDDIE: (VO)   Keep your legs crossed you dirty cow.

VAG: And I'm going to show you what alcoholics
                like to eat.

EDDIE: (VO)   Puss, puss, puss.

CLITTY: There are two kinds of alcoholics. Those
                that can't get enough to drink and those that
                can. If you're lucky enough to be in the
                second category you'll soon come across a
                problem that we all have to deal with sooner
                or later. Unconciousness. This can slow
                down your drinking. If you want to drink
                yourself to death, here is a helpful tip.

She produces a sewing needle.

                This is an ordinary sewing needle. When
                you feel unconciousness coming on, just ram
                it up under your fingernail, with a short
                jabbing motion.

VAG pours out a sherry.

VAG: Thanks Clitty. I expect you're wondering
                what do alcoholics eat? Naturally most of
                us would rather drink than eat, and to save
                valuable drinking time, many off-licences
                are now selling food. These are called
                supermarkets, and they carry a wide range of
                very fast foods. My favourite is instant
                smash.
Holds up packet.
                Just take one mouthful... and wash it down
                with a large weak scotch.
She demonstrates this.
                Ummm...delicious. And for the sweet, I
                suggest a couple of valium washed down with
                a large weak gin, will set you right for the
                evening.

CLITTY: And if you're not drinking alone?

VAG: Well for those special drinking occasions
                like your daughter's wedding, drown a nice
                plump turkey.

Produces live turkey.

VAG: ...in a pool of sherry.

Pours sherry over the turkey.

              Then pop it in the microwave. (she does)

CLITTY: Ummm, that looks delicious Vag. I think
              we both deserve a large scotch.

There is a loud crash.
                                        CUT TO:

EDDIE has fallen over and is foaming at the mouth.

EDDIE: Give me some scotch you bastards.

He tries to bite his way through the ropes.

                                        CUT TO:

DOUG and LIONEL with backs to camera studying two
posters on a wall.

LIONEL: Outstanding.

DOUG: A masterpiece.

LIONEL: A modern statement I should think.

DOUG: I agree it's the latest thing.

They turn and see the camera with mock surprise.

DOUG: Oh hello.

LIONEL: Hello again. Isn't modern art interesting.
              Here you have two modern painters. Both
              homosexuals. On the right we have a picture by
              America's Mr. Andy Warhol, and on the left
              another picture by our own Mr. David Hockney.

DOUG: Very nice.

LIONEL: Now if you look closely, you will notice
              that the Hockney is approximately a third
              of the size of the Warhol. But this one...
He points at the Hockney.
              costs more than this one. Now why is that?

DOUG: (Looks closely at the pictures)
              Well er... maybe it's because Hockney has --
              er -- you know, a richer colour sense, a
              more delicate line and -- er-- more palm trees.

LIONEL: That's exactly right Doug. Now this is
            where it gets interesting. You see Warhol
            wasn't slow to catch on. He soon tumbled
            to Hockney's game. It seemed like overnight,
            the wily Britisher had cornered the palm tree market

DOUG: So Hockney had him by the balls.

LIONEL: Briefly, yes. But Warhol wasn't done yet.
            He immediately set about making his pictures
            not only bigger but cheaper than Hockney's.

DOUG: How could he do that?

LIONEL: Mass production. By setting up an underground
            factory and reproducing his own pictures on
            the side, thereby undercutting Hockney.

DOUG: What a clever bastard.

LIONEL: Naturally, it wasn't long before Hockney
            tumbled his game and soon after that Warhol
            was found shot.

DOUG: Surprise, surprise.

CLITTY appears behind DOUG and LIONEL with a roll-up screen.

LIONEL: Alright Darling.

He winks at camera. DOUG winks too.

CLITTY: Eddie wants to show his slides.

DOUG: Oh, let me give you a hand.

They set up the screen.

LIONEL: Fancy a quick one down the Grevious Bodily
            Arms?

EDDIE: (VO) Not there stupid! Put it in the middle.

DOUG: Yeah -- with me as well. I'll come too.

CLITTY: I've got to help Eddie with his holiday
            slides.

EDDIE leers into a camera.

EDDIE: Holidays! Ha ha ha. Get it working you
            bastards.

LIONEL: How about the interval?

DOUG winks at the camera again.

EDDIE: (To camera)
              Hello. Holidays are mostly boring for me.
              If you go to the Norfolk Broads and you get
              on a boat, then you have miles and miles of
              wasteland between each pub. That's one
              kind of holiday. Some holidays like mountain
              climbing in Wales, you never get a decent
              reception on the telly. So I hate holidays
              like that and I always go to Clapham Junction
              for my holidays now, and I stay with Sinky
              de Brink. We like to de-rail a few trains
              and have a good laugh. However, you get
              bored though doing the same thing every year
              don't you? Well, you do. This year I got
              myself interested in aeroplanes. Sometimes
              aeroplanes will crash for no reason at all.
              So for this year's holiday, I went to Heathrow
              Airport on the off chance.

He turns to the others. VAG in the meantime has been
propping the slide projector up with telephone directories.

              Ready! Go!

EDDIE presses the remote control button. A picture of
Heathrow Airport appears on the screen.

              Ha ha ha! Heathrow Airport, International and
              seemingly safe.

PICTURE 2:   The road tunnel entrance to Heathrow.

              This is the entrance to Heathrow airport.
              Gateway to the world's Duty Free Shops.

PICTURE 3.   EDDIE leaning against the information desk
talking to a girl behind it.

              This is the information desk. And that's
              a woman that I'm asking if there's been any
              crashes today. But there isn't.

PICTURE 4.   EDDIE on balcony with binoculars.

              Here I am in the Queen's Building watching
              the runway in the hope of spotting tell-tale
              skid marks or bits of wreckage left behind in
              the smoke and chaos.

PICTURE 5.   EDDIE drinking at a bar. The barman is
              watching him.

Bit quiet around here isn't it, I'm saying to this barman.

PICTURE 6.   EDDIE whispering in barman's ear and waving a pound note.

This is me whispering to him and offering him money if he can tell me where I can get some souvenir wreckage.

PICTURE 7:   BARMAN telling EDDIE to fuck off.

I don't think he knew anything.

PICTURE 8:   EDDIE putting a packet of cigarettes in his pocket.

This is me stealing some fags.

PICTURE 9:   EDDIE under a clock.

This is the main airport clock. This clock goes non stop for twenty four hours and is looked at by people of all nationalities.

PICTURE 10:   EDDIE smoking.

Still no luck so far.

PICTURE 11:   EDDIE at the Lufthansa desk doing a Nazi salute.

Here I am chatting up some German girls.

PICTURE 12:   EDDIE drinking in the bar.

Time for a break.

PICTURE 13:   EDDIE listening to an airplane pilot's heart and giving a thumbs up.

This is an aeroplane pilot with a possible heart condition.

PICTURE 14:   EDDIE poking the pilot in the eye with his finger.

Here I am trying to wind him up and bring on a heart attack.

PICTURE 15:   EDDIE fleeing down the escalator.

Who is that hunk. It's Eddie Monsoon. Amateur Disaster Enthusiast... Ha ha ha.

PICTURE 16:   Middle East businessman with briefcase.

This is an Arab with a bomb.

PICTURE 17:   Plane taking off.

And this is the plane he took off in.

PICTURES 18/19/20:
The same place at different stages off take-off.

PICTURE 21:   The plane is a speck in the sky.

This is the same plane safely in air.
What a let down.

PICTURE 22:   EDDIE in the bar.

This is me getting pissed again.

PICTURE 23:   EDDIE outside ladies toilet.

And hanging around outside the ladies toilet.

PICTURE 24:   A corridor. Security guard in foreground.

Down that passageway is where they keep the
Duty Free. Ha ha.

PICTURE 25: AIR HOSTESS coming out of ladies toilet.
EDDIE is talking to her.

How many near crashes have you been in,
I'm asking this pretty air hostess from Uganda.

PICTURE 26:   Plane on the runway.

Another plane that didn't crash land.

PICTURE 27:   A crowd of people waiting with signs like
'Embassy Hotel', 'Greenway Tours', 'Upton
College' etc.

These are people touting for business from
passengers who are tired and emotional.

PICTURE 28:   EDDIE (in crowd) with placard saying:
'Go down on Eddie tours.'

PICTURE 29:   EDDIE is talking to a girl with a huge
rucksack. He has his arms in the air.

This is Jean from Sheffield, who is about
to fly to Teneriffe. Her first time in
an aeroplane. She is very nervous. Here
I am telling her about the famous air crashes
there.

PICTURE 30:   Close-up of JEAN in tears.

This is JEAN again. I wouldn't mind giving her one. If she ever gets back.

PICTURE 31:   Heathrow Airport at dusk.

Heathrow Airport again. This picture was taken at opening time.

PICTURE 32:   Another picture of the Airport at dusk.

Another nice picture. Here the airport looks black and dangerous... or is it?

PICTURE 33:   EDDIE beside a sign saying Heathrow Airport.

Goodbye Heathrow -- see you next year.
And that's the end of my holiday. Lights!

DOUG: That was very nice, Eddie.

VAG: Yes, I felt like I was there.

LIONEL: (At the drinks cabinet) Sherry anybody.

EDDIE: (Pacing up and down with excitement) Oh, I've got loads more than that to show you.
(He swigs some Scotch)
What's next on my television show! Where's the list!

CLITTY: (Taking a sherry from LIONEL) Here.

EDDIE: Quick, give it to me!

She fumbles.

Come on quickly, before those bastard adverts start!

He snatches it from her.

DOUG: There's still two minutes to go, Eddie.

EDDIE: Shut up! Where are we. Where are we. Er, Warhol, Hockney, Eddie's holiday... letters!
Where are the letters?

VAG: You've got them.

EDDIE: I gave them to you, nymphomaniac. Oh,
                here they are.

                        He gets them out of his back
                        pocket, leers at camera.

                Ha ha ha. Here are some viewer's letters
                with problems.

                        He sits down.

                Dear Eddie. This is a good one. 'I am
                happily married with two children, but three
                years ago at the office Christmas party I
                had sexual relations with my boss. Although
                the brief affair was quite short and didn't
                last very long, I still feel guilty. What
                should or shall I do. Please don't read
                my name out. Yours.'

                        He looks closely.

                Mary Bryant. Twenty-seven Acorn Drive.
                Lionel?

LIONEL: Umm. I think the most practical
                advice I can give to you Mary, is that
                you find out everything you possibly can
                about your boss's past and, er, when
                you've done that, blackmail him. I think
                you'll find that a re-enactment of the
                affair in the presence of a photographer
                will be a great help. Because let's face
                it, blackmail is not always as easy as it
                sometimes looks.

EDDIE: Doug?

DOUG: Well I think this is the most disgusting
                thing I've ever heard. It really is. All
                I can say is, I wouldn't let a whore like
                you feed my children.

EDDIE: Vag?

VAG: Yes well this is obviously a personal dig
                at me, because you know perfectly well I
                met my late husband at an office romp.
                I find this kind of letter extremely
                offensive and I hope you get herpes.

EDDIE: (Swigs from a bottle) I think the answer's
                easy. (Burps) Don't make a mountain out
                of a molehill Mary. Tell your husband
                everything. Shoot the children, then emigrate.

CLITTY: Well I think you're all being very hard
           on Mary Bryant and I think...

EDDIE: Here's a funny one. Dear Eddie, recently
           my father died. His pet dog Chippy is so
           mournful, we don't know what to do with
           him. Ha ha ha. Vag.

VAG: Death is a very difficult time for all of
           us and I know that a loved one is
           irreplaceable but have you tried oral
           sex.

DOUG: I think prior to having Chippy destroyed
           and sent to Jesus you should examine the
           will very carefully because Chippy may be
           the sole beneficiary. I mean how big's
           the dog?

LIONEL: No I think before you put the dog down
           you should check that the father really
           is dead. Because if he isn't and the dog's
           dead. The shock could kill him.

CLITTY: I'm sorry but I think vag's got it totally
           wrong again. In my experience oral sex,
           especially with animals, doesn't solve
           anything. I think it is extremely dangerous
           and can lead to severe tooth decay.

EDDIE: (Checking his teeth) That's all bollocks.
           Just stick a banger up his arse and give
           him the key to the drinks cabinet.

           Here's a good one.

           'Dear Eddie. I have a problem with men.
           All I seem to get is one night stands. I
           seem unable to develop any kind of meaningful
           relationship with a man.'

VAG: What's the matter? You're getting it aren't
           you? If you want a meaningful relationship,
           get a dog.

CLITTY: Yes you seem to be one of those girls that
           rhymes with apple tart.

LIONEL: The way I see it is this. If a girl is pretty
           and attractive, she gets it a lot. And
           I think that as you've been over-penetrated
           you're obviously unfit for marriage. I
           suggest you become an alcoholic.

EDDIE: From your letter I can deduce you've obviously
           got big tits. So why don't you spread it
           round a bit.

DOUG: Yeah, what's the name and address.

EDDIE: Here's another one. 'Dear Eddie...'

               "END OF PART ONE" APPEARS on the
               SCREEN. LIONEL gets up.

LIONEL: Let's pop round the pub.

EDDIE: Sit down you bastards, we haven't finished...

                        PART TWO

A proscenium with curtains closed. A fanfare PLAYS and
the curtains open to reveal EDDIE's head. It is in fact
a head'sized theatre and EDDIE's face takes up the entire
stage.

EDDIE: Thank you. I will now, with completely no
               assistance, not even a garage -- I will
               now remove one of my eyeballs. Maybe
               this one or maybe not this one. Who can
               tell? I shall then insert it in my catapult
               and I shall hire it up. Yes I said up my
               nose, whereupon ladies it will miraculously
               reappear in the socket from whence it came.
               Either this one (winks) or this one (winks).
               So long as I sniff hard enough. As you can
               maybe imagine, this is a very stupid and
               dangerous thing to do, so before attempting
               it I shall drink this bottle of formaldehyde.
               Before I attempt this feat, let me issue
               the following warning to any children who
               may be watching this programme.

                   He looks close up at the camera lens.

               Look out!!

               Right music please!

                   The MUSIC STARTS. He drinks the
                   entire bottle of formaldehyde and
                   smacks his lips. He smiles at the
                   camera, then collapses out of sight.

               Get those alligators out of here.

                   CUT TO VAG pouring out a sherry.

VAG: A lot of career girls these days are finding
            that more and more they are under pressure
            to put big things in their mouths. If
            you've got a few minutes to spare each
            day try practising with a telephone.

                    She puts a telephone receiver in
                    her mouth. A thin voice from the
                    receiver says: "Hello, hello"

                    CUT TO LIONEL facing camera. Behind
                    him DOUG and CLITTY are sitting round
                    the coffee table.

LIONEL: Hello again viewers. Here's a little piece
            called: 'I'm not sleeping with both of you.

CLITTY: You get this straight, Douglas and Lionel
            Prescott. I'm not sleeping with both of you.

DOUG: Sleep? No we just want to do intercourse
            with you.

LIONEL: (At the drinks cabinet) Sherry Diana?

CLITTY: What, so I'll drink all night and won't
            know what I'm doing?

                    Takes drink.

LIONEL: Let me just captain the situation as I see
            it. We've been drinking now since seven
            o'clock. And by about ten o'clock we start
            to get a stiffy.

CLITTY: A what?

DOUG: A stiffy.

CLITTY: A stiffy?

DOUG: Yeah -- a stiffy.

LIONEL: Yes. Now usually on a Saturday night we can
            be almost certain to get a couple of birds
            who will have intercourse with us. Do you
            follow what I'm saying?

CLITTY: Oh I know what your game is. Physical
            pleasure.

DOUG: Good. Now we're getting somewhere.

LIONEL: However tonight, the young lady that Doug
            was buying drinks for... For some unknown
            reason didn't want to do it with Doug. Now
            without being personal, Diana, you are a
            tramp and everybody knows it!

CLITTY: Yes, yes, maybe I am a nymphomaniac and
             can't get enough of it, but I really don't
             like either of you.

DOUG: That's all right, we don't like you.

CLITTY: I mean you must admit you're both quite
             ugly and I'm starting to sober up.

LIONEL: More sherry, Diana?

DOUG: You're no bleedin' oil painting yourself.

LIONEL: Hold on, hold on. Let's recap the situation.
             We've all had a lovely night out and
             what with the drinks, the chicken in the
             basket and the forty Embassy, you've set
             me back about thirteen pounds. So technically
             you're with me. Am I being fair?

DOUG: Yes, so what's your answer Diana? Are you
             going to sleep with both of us or not.

CLITTY: I can see now that it's all over. You've
             won me over you smooth talking bastards.
             You've ensnared me in your web of slimy
             innuendo and the woman in me can't take it
             anymore. Yes, let's have our night of fun
             in my hideaway love-nest. Once again a
             girl from a broken home seeks affection
             only to become a victim of her unnatural
             sex urge that leads to an orgy of all night
             drinking sessions and wild sex romps.

             DOUG and LIONEL look at each other.
             Silence.

LIONEL: Sherry, Doug?

             The door opens. EDDIE bursts in with
             the MYSTERY GUEST. He has a paper bag
             over his head with a hole cut for the
             mouth.

EDDIE: Right, stand there! Mr. Mystery Guest!

             EDDIE runs to the settee. VAG joins
             them.

             Right. Go!

GUEST: I'm twenty-four. I'm single. I was born
             under the sign of Leo and I'm a member of
             an ethnic minority.

EDDIE: Ha ha. Hard one this.

CLITTY: Are you an Eskimo?

GUEST: No I'm not.

VAG: You say that you're single and born under
            the sign of Leo. Are you a racing driver?

GUEST: No. But I wish I was.

EDDIE: Er, d'you take speed?

GUEST: Yes I do.

DOUG: Have you got any on you now?

GUEST: No I haven't.

LIONEL: Are you an ex-porn merchant supergrass?

GUEST: No I'm not.

EDDIE: Yes I know -- I know. Are you... Are you
            a cowardly, drug peddling Irish bomber
            dwarf, ha ha ha.

            The others laugh.

GUEST: No I'm not.

DOUG: I've got it. You're an insolent, job
            snatching evil spastic train driving Aslef
            bastard!

GUEST: No I'm not.

VAG: Are you an ungrateful, dole scrounging
            glue-sniffing nurse/health worker?

GUEST: Er... no.

LIONEL: Ah I know. You're a balding, commie, child-
            molesting, chain smoking, ballot rigging,
            vegetarian, bastard, leader of the GLC?

GUEST: No I'm not.

CLITTY: Are you an unrepentant black homosexual?

GUEST: Yes I am.

            LOUD APPLAUSE. GUEST takes off
            hood.

EDDIE: Ladies and gentlemen. Mr. Alan Pellay.

                MORE APPLAUSE. He kicks DOUG.

                Come on you, got to go now.

DOUG: What?

EDDIE: This is the big interview. So clear off
                you bastards.

                They leave.

                Where d'you want to sit, Alan? On the
                chair or the settee. If you have the chair,
                you have to sit on your own.

ALAN: Oh I really don't mind, love.

                He sits on the chair.

EDDIE: Now question number one, Alan. What most
                people want to know about homos is what do
                they do in their spare time. You know,
                hobbies and things.

ALAN: Well I like reading and er...

                He gets up and picks up a full
                ashtray.

                D'you mind if I clear this up. It's just
                that dirt attracts ghosts and demons.
                I've seen it happen, love.

                He clears up as he's talking.

EDDIE: Oh good idea. Yes some people say I smell
                Alan, but I never mention it. What d'you
                think?

ALAN: Well I don't think a bar of soap and a tub
                of water would go amiss.

EDDIE: Sometimes I smell even worse than I do now.

ALAN: Look love, deep down everybody's the same.
                We're all shit really, aren't we.

EDDIE: That's what I think. They're all bastards.

ALAN: Umm.

                EDDIE takes a swig. Pause.

EDDIE: Right, er... question number two. What's
                the worst thing that ever happened to you?
                Being born a wog or a poof?

ALAN: Well, Eddie.

EDDIE: Or maybe they're both as bad as each other.
         What d'you think. Go ahead, be as
         technical as you like.

ALAN: Well anybody who knows me, Eddie, will
         tell you that I'm -- that I'm very happy
         with both my race and my sexuality.
         You know, like I don't think I'd be any
         happier being white or a girl or anything.

EDDIE: What, not even Raquel Welch?

ALAN: Oh no.

EDDIE: Oh come on, Alan. If you were Raquel Welch
         you could be screwing Burt Reynolds or
         somebody really famous.

ALAN: There's more to life than Burt Reynolds,
         believe me.

EDDIE: Who then? Roger Moore, James Caan? Let's
         have some names. Who's sticking it up who?

ALAN: No Eddie, I'm through with all that. You
         know like the whole fake fag hag scene.
         Like I don't want to talk about David
         Bowie, you know... and I'm not going to
         talk about Garry Glitter or Elton. You
         know like Elton wanted me to be Lucy in
         the sky with diamonds... you know like he
         does a big number on it and he wanted me
         to come down on a swing you know... like
         with all me sequins and veils. You know,
         and like I was Lucy. That was like the
         climax of the show -- a really big number
         but like I won't do that now. I'm just
         not going to do that big drag queen number.
         I just want to be me now. Like I won't
         regress unless it's for -- you know, big
         money. Like the Damned asked me to
         introduce them at the Hammersmith Odeon.
         I said I wanted a thousand pounds if I'm
         going to regress in front of those thugs.

EDDIE: So what do you do now then, Alan? Are
         you into some new kind of perversion?

ALAN: Well, Eddie, it depends what you mean
         by new?

EDDIE: Well you know, do you still like kissing
         blokes on the mouth and things like that?

ALAN: It's funny you should say that, Eddie,
             but one of the things I really hate is
             when they stick their tongues down your
             throat. It really turns me off.

EDDIE: Yeah me too.

ALAN: Funny isn't it.

EDDIE: This is where we stop talking now, Alan,
             because it's the end of the Eddie Monsoon
             interview.

ALAN: Well it's been wonderful, Eddie.

EDDIE: You see we've got these two women now,
             who are going to show the viewers how to
             beat up men who rape women by having
             intercourse and sex and using force
             against their will at closing time.

                  CUT TO CLOSEUP of VAG's face.

VAG: Many alcoholics get into fights at closing
             time. This is because after a heavy
             night's drinking, the alcoholic quite
             understandably hates everybody. When
             this intense feeling appears, the quickest
             form of relief is called 'Hitting Out.'
             To do this you must first go into the
             Ladies toilet and change into one of these.

                  CAMERA PULLS BACK SHOWING VAG
                  dressed in protective padding.
                  With helmet and holding a spiked
                  club.

             Now you are ready for the brawl. Clitty
             is very kindly going to help me in this
             demonstration.

CLITTY: Well I'll do my best. (Smiles)

VAG: The best thing is to hit out first while
             the bitch still has a drink in her hand.

                  She smashes a bottle over CLITTY's
                  head.

             Or, failing that, hit her in the stomach on
             her way to the toilet.

                  She hits CLITTY in the stomach with
                  the spiked club.

VAG: (CONT'D) Now that you've attracted her attention,
you are ready to start brawling in earnest, and
should get a few vicious blows in before
the police arrive. Here are some of them.

You can try biting her ear off, one of my
favourites. Or a finger in the ear
followed by a knee in the crotch.

She demonstrates these on CLITTY.

Then stamp on her foot and hit the drunken
cow in the face.

CLITTY falls over unconscious.

Now that you've filled her in, here are
some ladylike ways of passing out.

VAG does a series of falls. CUT TO:

EDDIE sitting at the piano.

EDDIE: I am now going to play the piano and sing
a song, but not necessarily in that order.
Seeing as it's February, I thought I'd do
one about last year. Nineteen Eighty-Two
was a pile of pooh. Especially if you
didn't make it through. Like Grace Kelly
and Arthur Lowe, Harry H. Corbett and
probably Sooty as well, Ingrid Bergman,
Arthur Askey, Leonid Brezhnev and the Queen
Mother.

To know what happened in
Nineteen Eighty-Two
All you've got to do is read the papers.
In July the obituary column
was only three inches long.
There was quite an interesting article
on homosexual policemen.
Some people thought that bus fares
were too high.
There was that Hell's Angel who wanted
to kill his wife's lover with a bomb.
Richard Shilgoe sang a song about only
being able to buy screws in
packets of four.
Keep up the good work Richard.

He stops singing and notices a piece
of glass on the floor.

Wait a minute! There's a piece of glass on
the floor.

Deadly hush.

EDDIE: Hey! I said there's a piece of glass on
              the floor, you bastards!

                   Listens to his earphone.

              Yes I know it's a small piece of glass,
              but so's your cock.

                   Listens again and moves closer to
                   the camera.

              Excuse me ladies and gentlemen, I'm talking
              to the producer, so mind your own business
              for a while.

              Look Bob, I know I've got shoes on but
              supposing we had a troupe of Maori Dancers
              in -- heh?

                   Listens.

              Look, just because they can walk on fire
              doesn't mean they can walk on glass does it.

                   Listens.

              No it doesn't.

                   Listens.

              Oh so you've definitely seen them do it
              have you? Well when was the last time
              you were in Africa?

                   Listens.

              All right, New Zealand then! Bastards.
              Where was I? Who cares. Look, the best
              thing that happened last year was the
              Falklands. It's just a pity we didn't
              send two para to the world cup.

              But here's a quick look at a few things
              that might brighten up 1983.

                   He sings again.

              Factory. Farming
              Repatriation
              Capital punish
              ment in schools
              Labour camps
              for the unemployed
              Death penalty
              for old age shoplifters

EDDIE: (Singing)

                Hanging Australians
                Five gold things.
                A bit more Argie Bargie
                French Exocets
                Right up their bums
                And Scotch on the National

                        He repeats last line several times.
                        The others appear, singing the last
                        line. VAG is wheeling on the turkey,
                        now black like charcoal. LIONEL has
                        a tray of sherry.

EDDIE: That was a great song Eddie.

LIONEL: Sherries all round I think.

EDDIE: Bring on all the gear.

LIONEL: Well that was a great show, Eddie. I
                thought the darkie was very good.

DOUG: Show business, phew.

CLITTY: Yes, showbusiness, phew.

VAG: (Cutting the turkey) Next week, I'll
                be showing you how your husband should
                be hung.

                        Holds up a noose.

                With one of these.

CLITTY: And I'll be starting with embalming for
                beginners.

VAG: Leg or feathers, Doug?

LIONEL: Next week we'll be showing you some of
                the new Prescott Sunshine Retirement
                Villas for the old and vulnerable.

EDDIE: I'll be talking about necrophillia
                with Willy Whitelaw and taking an
                in-depth look at Jewish persecution
                during World War Two. Did it really
                happen?

DOUG: And also I'll be miming to Johnny Mathis'
                latest single.

LIONEL: Umm. I'll be looking forward to that.

EDDIE: What a lot we'll all be doing. Well
              that's the end of the show. Hope you'll
              be tuning in next week, when we'll be
              getting -- back to normal!

ALL: Back to normal.

                   They all shout and jump up and
                   down, shouting "Party Time. Music!"

              "THE END"

Written by Adrian Edmondson, Dawn French, Nigel Planer,
Peter Richardson, Peter Richens and Jennifer Saunders

Starring:

EDDIE MONSOON   VAG

DOUG PRESCOTT   CLITTY

LIONEL PRESCOTT   ALAN PELLAY

Directed by Bob Spiers